TRAVEL READY
PACKING

Pack Light • Dress Right

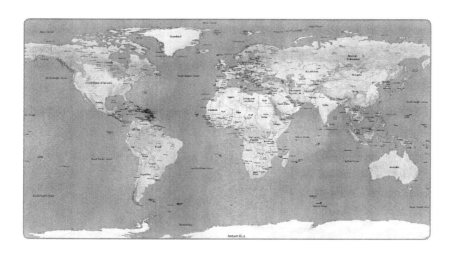

Anytime, Anywhere

Based on Climate, Culture, Type of Trip and Gender

Julie Ann Martin

TRAVEL-READY PACKING: Pack Light, Dress Right—Anytime, Anywhere
by Julie Ann Martin

Argo & Cole Publishers
439 North Larchmont Blvd.
Los Angeles, California 90004
Fax: 323/464-5608
E-mail: publisher@argocole.net
Web site: travelreadypacking.com
E-mail: julie@travelreadypacking.com

ISBN: 978-0-9791186-1-6
Library of Congress Control Number: 2009929755

10 9 8 7 6 5 4 3 2 1

Book Design by SUN Editing & Book Design, suneditwrite.com

Printed and bound in the United States of America

Disclaimer: The information in this book is accurate at the time of publishing. Travel-Ready Packing is based on general weather conditions, which are subject to changes beyond our control. Because weather is variable, Travel-Ready Packing cannot be responsible for unseasonal weather conditions at a given destination. It is advisable to check the forecast before beginning your trip.

TRAVEL-READY PACKING

Pack Light • Dress Right
Anytime, Anywhere

This book is dedicated to my mother who sponsored many trips, taught me how to minimize, supported all my adventures — no matter how dangerous or bizarre, and has watched me pack so many times through the years.

Table of Contents

Introduction

Traveling is exciting but what if you can't find a place to stay? What if it's difficult to get a taxi? What if you need to change hotels because you don't like the one you're in? What if you have to pay lots of extra baggage fees? These are just some of the reasons to travel light.

Traveling light is not easy, but once you understand how it works, it alleviates most travel frustrations.

In our consumer-oriented society, many of us fill our lives with useful devices, important things, and usually lots of clothes. Our identities become entangled with our possessions. We can't imagine ourselves without our stuff. When traveling, I take a break from my stuff. I pack only what's necessary and useful. This is the art of packing light, and it's difficult to master. You need to conquer the "What if" questions. How? Know what to expect. If you have been to France several times, you probably know exactly what to pack. But you may not have known what to pack on your first trip.

When you go on vacation, you want to leave your troubles behind. Why burden yourself by packing your entire wardrobe? Believe it or not, what you pack determines how enjoyable your holiday will be. By traveling light, you will experience an inexplicable freedom and be relaxed and comfortable, open to enjoy new adventures.

You can experience the freedom of traveling light before leaving home. If you are a woman, try leaving your purse at home for a couple days or even a week. Put your money and other necessary items in a secure pocket, and go. You will be slightly uncomfortable at first, but you will find that you have discovered a new kind of freedom. This is mostly the freedom associated with breaking old habits. This is what you do when you travel. You leave your daily routine behind. Leave your car at home for a day or a week. Take a taxi, train, bus or walk. There is even more freedom to be experienced in these activities. Freedom, after all, is the essence of travel.

"Your clothes are your wings." This Korean proverb applies to packing your suitcase as well as how you present yourself to the world. If you present yourself in an appropriate manner while traveling, your hosts will treat you better. This mutual respect welcomes harmony with the environment and culture. You feel less awkward and encounter fewer difficulties in a foreign location.

Dressing appropriately means tailoring your wardrobe according to social and cultural norms. In other words, showing respect to the people who live in the area you are visiting. It's important to not call unnecessary attention to yourself. You certainly don't want to be easily recognized as a tourist who is potentially carrying a lot of money.

For example, in conservative regions, women should pay careful attention to their sleeve and skirt lengths. Even in extremely hot places, you can wear long sleeves if you choose the right fabric. In some Asian countries, wearing a tank top is like walking around topless. You certainly wouldn't walk around topless in New York City so don't do it in Asian cities.

When selecting a travel wardrobe, the two major factors to consider are weather and culture. Some countries have extremely hot or cold climates, so special fabrics are required to maintain comfort. Some cultures have stricter social rules so appropriate clothing is necessary to enjoy your travels.

TRAVEL-READY PACKING: Pack Light, Dress Right—Anytime, Anywhere is your reference guide for all your future destinations. Enjoy your journeys!

— Julie Ann Martin
Travel-Ready Packing
2009

How to Use this Book

Note

The new regulation size for carry-ons varies from airline to airline. The usual size allowed is 22"x 14"x 9"—Maximum size is 45 linear inches. You will need to check with your carrier. Also, be aware that if you plan to always carry your bag onto the airplane, you will need to comply with the liquids restrictions. You can check updates via www.travelreadypacking.com.

Table of Contents

Consult the Table of Contents (pages 7–12) or the Index of Destinations (pages 165–169) for area or country destinations.

Weather

Consult the weather charts within each section. Remember that these charts depict general climates. Day to day weather can vary.

Wardrobe

Consult the corresponding wardrobe for the season you will be visiting. Some climates have different seasons, but do not require an extensive change in wardrobes. Some destinations require a completely different pack depending on the season.

Accessories

There is a separate accessory list that applies to all destinations.

Rationale

The rationales provided will help you to decide whether or not to bring certain items.

Styles

Each wardrobe chart includes a definition of the styles required in specific regions. At the end of each regional section and just after the recommended packing lists, there are some tips concerning style and cultural wardrobe considerations.

Below is a chart that defines the terms used when describing regional norms.

STYLE MODE—HOW STYLISH IS YOUR DESTINATION?	ATTITUDE—WHAT ARE THE LOCAL CUSTOMS IN REGARD TO DRESS CODES?
Casual: Tourists and locals do not wear dressy clothing. The choice is yours.	**Liberal:** There are no social restrictions concerning sleeve and skirt lengths or styles of attire.
Moderate: Tourists and locals wear fashionable yet functional attire. Shorts and T-shirts are too casual.	**Moderate:** There are some social restrictions concerning fashion. To fit in, choose nicer clothing.
Dressy: These are more cosmopolitan areas where people dress up on a daily basis. The traveler does not need to wear formal clothing, but should choose appropriate styles.	**Conservative:** There are strict social restrictions concerning sleeve and skirt lengths and styles of clothing that should not be ignored. Women will need long sleeves, pants, long blouses over pants (covering the hips), and longer skirts.

Safety

The general safety level for each region is listed after the regional packing chart.

Low	Safety and security of the traveler is variable and the area could be dangerous. Precautions should be taken.
Moderate	Travelers should be aware that there is the possibility of dangerous situations and possible crime. Precautions should be taken.
High	Safety in these regions is generally good. The crime rates are low, but some precautions should still be taken.

Choosing Clothes

The items suggested in these lists are the basics. A pair of pants can be formal, casual, or dressy. Your choice will depend on your personal preference and the style recommendations following each packing list.

Types of Trips

The lists are designed for trips from one week and up to six months. Additional lists have been provided for the adventure traveler, multiple-climate destinations, the expatriate, and the around the world backpacker. For the business traveler, the travel packing lists are season-specific.

A Brief Discussion about Culture

The following definitions and explanations are intended to serve as guidelines to help you gain insight into the complexity of cultures. Cultural considerations are important. Superior and inferior cultures do not exist. There are just differences. Understanding a foreign culture lessens frustration thus making your trip more enjoyable.

As a simple definition, culture is the learned patterns of thought and behavior of a group or society of people who have created rules for living from generation to generation.

Culture encompasses every aspect of how a society has evolved and dictates social rules. Culture involves how people interact with each other, what food they eat, what clothes they wear, and what language they speak. Social rules, the way people do things in cultures, are often the most perplexing issues for outsiders. Visitors often find themselves saying, "Why do they do it that way?" Usually cultural reasons link behavior patterns that are invisible to the casual traveler.

The best rule of thumb for travelers, who are annoyed by cultural differences they can't grasp, is not to view one's own culture as being superior. Accept the differences and adapt. We do not travel so we can sit in judgment of people. We travel so we can appreciate and learn from diversity.

Within cultures, there are sub-cultures. Not all people in a culture are the same in every way although sub-culture's beliefs, patterns of behavior and language, share many similarities with the main culture. For example, New Yorkers are quite different from Californians while both are very different to people in America's Deep South, yet all speak English and are Americans.

*TRAVEL-READY PACKING'*s cultural perspectives are based on general characteristics stemming from the main culture of the country or region. Understanding a bit about the main culture will help you adapt to your foreign destination. Keep in mind that there is also a difference in what you've been told about a culture, and how a culture really is. The best way to learn about a culture is to go there and see for yourself what it's like. For example, you will be surprised that many people around the world think most everyone in the United States is white, rich, and beautiful, and choose to carry guns and shoot each other day and night in city streets.

All of us are born into a culture that teaches us how to socialize, how to behave with others. We become comfortable in our own environments and fearful of change. Travelers will often seek out familiar fast food restaurants like McDonald's or Pizza Hut, not just for the familiar food, but also to feel more relaxed in the foreign environment.

Traveling is a change, and the traveler becomes the outsider. It's normal for the traveler to dislike how other people are acting. When we are uncomfortable, we look for what is comfortable. What is comfortable is what we know, our own culture. Even with awareness of cultural differences, it's difficult to get past subconscious judgments.

Our behavior has been formed by our own culture, but may be inappropriate in foreign cultures. Even when there is no malicious intent, cross-cultural interactions can be insulting. For example, an excited traveler to Brazil may try to show appreciation to a Brazilian by making the O.K. sign with his fingers. The Brazilian sees this as an insult because in Brazil, this gesture means, in a vulgar sense, buzz off.

The clothes we wear can also be unintentionally insulting to the people in the host culture. Based on what you are wearing, locals will subconsciously approve or disapprove of you. The solution is simple. Select your wardrobe according to cultural considerations. This does not mean you must wear local garb. Rather dress appropriately for the situation. You will be treated better and enjoy your experience much more. This is not always difficult. In many cities around the world, you will be surprised that the norm is jeans or pants and a T-shirt, or jeans or pants and a good shirt. Often local, traditional clothing appears only on special holidays.

When referencing climatic wardrobe suggestions, pay attention to recommended sleeve lengths, skirt lengths, and types of pants.

Climate & Weather

What is the difference between climate and weather? Climate is general weather over a long period of time, or the average weather in a given place. Weather varies from day to day, some days it rains, some days it's sunny.

Latitude influences climate. The amount of sunlight is a prime cause of heat, so how far a region is north or south of the equator determines its climate. Equally important to climate are the speed and direction of the winds, the amount of rain that falls, and the local topography such as large bodies of water and mountains. These factors can cause major weather changes from what the latitude would suggest. Thus, there are also sub-climates and micro-climates.

Wladimir Koppen classified climates into five major categories: tropical, dry, mild, continental and polar.

1. Tropical

   Constantly high, hot temperatures. In some areas the high temperatures are accompanied by up to 240 inches of rain each year. The resulting vegetation is the tropical rain forest or jungle. Transitional areas bordering the rainy tropics north and south have distinct dry winter seasons. The Savanna in Africa is a good example of a transitional area.

2. Dry

   Very hot and dry. Dry climates make up about 30% of the Earth's land area. The Sahara, the Gobi, and the Australian deserts are examples of dry climates. In these climates rain is rare and temperatures are high. There are two sub-types, deserts and steppes. Steppes separate arid regions from wetter areas.

3. Mild

   Three groups: humid-subtropical, marine west coast, and Mediterranean.

   • Humid subtropical climates are influenced by air found over the oceans in the summer. The Southeastern United States has this type of climate: hot, humid summers and chilly to mild winters.

   • Marine west coast climates have mild winters and cool summers resulting from a constant inland flow of air over an ocean that has cold currents. These climates have abundant rain.

   • Mediterranean climates are warm and mild with hot summers influenced by the Mediterranean Sea, which has no cold currents.

4. Continental Climates

   Extremes in both heat and cold. Tropical and polar air masses meet and battle for dominance. The resulting weather can be severe. These areas have rapid changes in weather conditions. Both summer and winter can be extreme. The presence of warm, moist air can cause summers to be wetter than winters. Three sub-type summer climates exist in this category: summers which are warm, cool or sub-arctic. Natives living in these climates may explain, "If you don't like the weather, wait a few minutes and it will change."

5. Polar Climates

Constantly cold. Polar climates are north of continental climates. These are the opposite of the tropical climates. The average temperature for the warmest month is 10 Celsius, 40 Fahrenheit. Rain is generally low because the cold air is not able to hold much moisture. This type of climate can be found anywhere on earth if the altitude is high enough. The top of Kilimanjaro, near the equator, is a microclimate of an alpine setting.

Microclimates

These areas differ from the surrounding area. The climate of a small area can be quite different than the surrounding area because of the presence of water, such as an oasis in the desert; or the presence of topographic features, such as mountains and lakes. In general, as altitude increases, the temperature cools.

TRAVEL-READY PACKING: Pack Right, Dress Light—Anytime, Anywhere's weather charts depict the average weather in a given region. Seasonal and daily fluctuations often occur. These charts provide a general guideline so you may determine the most appropriate wardrobe for your destination.

Fabrics

Fabrics Defined

In general, fabric is constructed from fibers that are drawn into thread and then woven together into cloth. In ancient times it was all done by hand, but these days machines complete the process. Synthetic fibers are made of petroleum products that are drawn into filaments. The filaments are combined into thread, which is then woven together. Finer threads create finer fabrics. Coarser threads produce coarser fabric. Therefore, thinner, loosely woven fabrics are good for hot climates and coarser fabrics are better for cold climates.

Microfibers are very small in diameter and resemble silk.

Synthetic fabrics are easy-care, quick drying, and wrinkle-resistant. Be careful, many synthetics can be hot because they are tightly woven.

Combined synthetic with other components, particularly with cotton, become more loosely woven. The fabric dries quickly and is much cooler to wear.

Hot Destinations

Chiffon: This is a flowing, light, transparent material that dries quickly and drapes well. Usually it's made of polyester or nylon.

Cool-Max™: This is cotton blended with polyester and loosely woven to allow air to pass through.

Cotton: This is a natural fabric that is soft and can provide warmth or cool comfort depending on the weight of the fabric. However, 100% cotton takes a long time to dry and must be ironed. When blended with other fibers, drying time and wrinkles are reduced.

Cotton/Lycra™: Lycra™ is a strong stretchable synthetic fabric. Small amounts of Lycra™ can make the cotton more durable and flexible.

Linen: This is the best fabric for hot and humid climates. It's light, it breathes, and it looks great. Linen is better than cotton in heat and humidity because cotton gets too wet and sticky. Linen protects from the sun and provides a form of shade. Some linen is now washable rather than dry clean only, and some are blends that avoid excessive wrinkling.

Cold Destinations

Flannel: This is a finish for a fabric. It's brushed and combed on top, and becomes very soft. Air is trapped among the surface fibers producing insulation. Drying time is a problem.

Fleece/Polartec™: This material has many varieties and has been produced from recycled plastic soda bottles. These bottles are petroleum based and are reheated to be reused. Fibers are drawn out and spun into thread. The thread becomes a heavy fleece that has tiny air holes and thus holds heat around the body.

Georgette: This is a heavier version of chiffon. Most of these are blends of polyesters. They have flow and substance and are used for dressier clothes. It's usually easy-care and quick drying.

Gore-Tex™: This fabric is a spin-off from the space program. It's another petroleum- based material. It's waterproof and now more breathable than earlier versions.

Microfleece: This is a variation of fleece fabric. Polartec™ can be bulky but microfleece takes less packing space and feels softer. The same amount of warmth can be achieved as a heavier fleece with the layering principle.

Nylon: This was the first synthetic fiber. Nylon is now used to make wool washable, to add strength to many other fibers, and provide coatings to produce a lightweight waterproof material.

Polyesters: These are synthetic fibers from high tech laboratories. Early materials were hot and bulky. Newer versions can imitate any type of fabric and add the properties of easy care and durability. These fibers are added in various quantities to produce custom-made characteristics for a specific material.

Rayon: Another of the early synthetics that has been vastly improved. It's not as durable or as easy-care as nylon or the polyesters. Blends with acetate are common, but can be too warm in hot climates.

Wool: A wonderful natural fiber that is great for cool or cold destinations. Many people are sensitive to wool because it can be scratchy, but new blends are less coarse. Nylon added to wool makes it washable. Wool insulates well and keeps both heat and cold away.

Hot & Cold Destinations

Microfibers: These are synthetic fibers which can imitate silk for texture and feel but are easy-care, quick drying, and lightweight. Microfibers are great for hot climates as well as cold climate layering.

Tencel™ / Lyocell™ : One of the first natural fibers produced with high-tech procedures. This is a great travel fabric. The fabric feels like heavy silk, but dries relatively quickly.

Fabric Guide

The following chart is a guideline of fabrics that work well in the designated climates. You may, of course, have your own personal preference.

If you choose the correct fabric for your destination, your clothes will not only look great when you arrive, but will also help you adjust better to the climate.

	Hot or Hot and Humid
	Warm
	Tropical Dry Season
	Tropical Wet Season
	Hot, Wet, Monsoon
	Very Cold
	Cold/Rain
	Cold
	Cool

How to Use This Chart

Find the climate icon that is closest to your destination's climate. Search for the fabrics most suited to the climates.

Fabric	Climates
Chiffon	
Cool-Max™	
Cotton	
Cotton Blends	
Light Cotton	
Cotton/Lycra™ Blend	
Flannel	
Fleece	
Georgette	
Gore-Tex™	
Linen	
Microfibers	Microfibers are appropriate in all climates. They can be easily layered.
Micro-fleece	

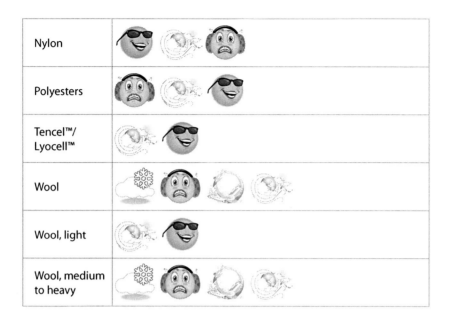

Nylon	
Polyesters	
Tencel™/ Lyocell™	
Wool	
Wool, light	
Wool, medium to heavy	

Travel in Muslim Countries

For traveling in Islamic countries in Asia, Indonesia, Africa and the Middle East, it's essential to know about Ramadan, a 28-day (lunar month) Muslim holiday. First, more conservative clothing is required. Second, availability of food and alcohol may be restricted. Third, tourist sites may have limited hours. During daylight hours, travelers are additionally required to refrain from eating, drinking or smoking cigarettes in the presence of Muslims.

From sunrise to sunset, Muslims fast – refrain from eating and drinking. In many Muslim countries, restaurants will be closed during the day. At sunset, Muslims break their fast and begin a night of festivities socializing with families and friends, as well as shopping. Often store and restaurant hours change day for night: closed during the day and open at sunset or an hour after sunset, staying open until 3 or 4 a.m. Non-food stores and government offices may also be open for fewer hours during the day.

Ramadan is a 28-day lunar month, so it occurs at different times each year. In 2010, it begins in the middle of August. In 2011, it begins at the beginning of August. In 2012, it will be mostly August. Check for exact dates before booking your trip since the dates are different every year.

Africa: Northwest

Algeria, Mali, Mauritania, Morocco, Tunisia, Western Sahara

Rain & Weather
There is hardly any rain in this region.

Best Time to Visit: December – April

Cultural considerations are very important. Desert sand is also of concern. Be sure to stuff a bandana into your pack to protect your face and head from the sun and blowing sand.

 ### Weather by Month

MONTH	GENERAL WEATHER CONDITIONS	EXTREME WEATHER WARNINGS
January		
February	Warm Days, Cool Nights	
March		
April		
May		DRY YEAR ROUND
June		
July		
August	Hot Days, Warm Nights	
September		
October		
November		
December	Warm Days, Cool Nights	

Africa: Northeast

Chad, Egypt, Libya, Niger

Rain & Weather

There is little concern for rain here. It's extremely hot June through August. Heat can be a concern year round. Please note that climates change in the middle of April and October.

Best Time to Visit: November – March

Cultural considerations are very important. Desert sand is also of concern. Be sure to stuff a bandana into your pack to protect your face and head from the sun and blowing sand.

 Weather by Month

MONTH	GENERAL	EXTREME WEATHER WARNINGS
January		
February	Warm, Dry	
March		
April 1–15	Warm, Dry	
16–30	Very Hot, Dry	
May		
June		DRY YEAR ROUND
July	Very Hot, Dry	
August		
September		
October 1–15	Very Hot, Dry	
16–31	Warm, Dry	
November	Warm, Dry	
December		

Africa: East & East Coast

Djibouti, Eritrea, Ethiopia, Kenya, Somalia, Sudan, Uganda

Rain & Weather

The south may have rain or drought from April to September. Nights can be cool. If traveling to the higher regions in Kenya, pack items for this cooler microclimate.

Best Time to Visit: January – March

 Weather by Month

MONTH	GENERAL	EXTREME WEATHER WARNINGS
January	Warm, Hot, Dry	
February		
March 1–15	Warm, Hot, Dry	
16–31	Warm, Rain	
April	Warm, Rain	
May		
June		HEAT YEAR ROUND
July	Warm, Hot, Dry	
August		
September		
October 1–15	Warm, Hot, Dry	
16–31	Warm, Rain	
November	Warm, Rain	
December		

Africa: Ivory Coast

Benin, Burkina Faso, Cote D'Ivoire,
Gambia, Ghana, Guinea, Guinea-
Bissau, Liberia, Senegal,
Sierra Leone, Togo

Rain & Weather

The rain can begin as early as March in the eastern region. The heaviest rainfall is April through June.

Best Time to Visit: December – April

Cultural considerations are important. Heat can also be a problem.

 Weather by Month

MONTH	GENERAL	EXTREME WEATHER WARNINGS
January	Hot, Dry	
February		
March 1–15	Hot, Dry	
16–31	Warm, Rain	
April 1–15	Hot, Dry	
16–30	Hot, Wet	
May		HEAT YEAR ROUND
June		
July	Hot, Wet	
August		
September		
October		
November	Hot, Dry	
December		

Africa: Central & Central Coast

Cameroon, Central African Republic,
Congo, Equatorial Guinea, Gabon,
Nigeria, Sao Tome, Principe

Rain & Weather

Rain is in the North from May to September, and in the South from October to April. This area is generally hot and humid year round with varying degrees of precipitation. There are also dry steppe climates and even desert climates in the south of the Central African Republic. Please consult the current local weather forecast before packing for your trip to ensure that you have rain gear if you need it.

Best Time to Visit

Northern Region: November – February
Southern Region: November – Late March

Cultural considerations are important. Heat can be a problem.

 Weather by Month

MONTH	GENERAL	EXTREME WEATHER WARNINGS
January		
February		
March		
April		
May		
June	Hot, Humid	HUMIDITY YEAR ROUND
July		
August		
September		
October		
November		
December		

Africa: Central East & West Coast

Angola, Burundi, Democratic
Republic of the Congo, Malawi,
Rwanda, Tanzania, Zambia

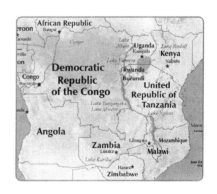

Rain & Weather

Rain is from November to March; the heaviest rainfall is from March to May.
It can get quite cool at higher elevations.

Best Time to Visit: June – August

Depending on your itinerary, a Multiple Climate pack, page 141, may be necessary.

 Weather by Month

MONTH	GENERAL WEATHER CONDITIONS	EXTREME WEATHER WARNINGS
January		
February	Hot, Wet	
March		
April		
May		
June		VARIABLE YEAR ROUND
July	Hot	
August		
September		
October		
November	Hot, Wet	
December		

Africa: South

Botswana, Lesotho,
Mozambique, Namibia, South
Africa, Swaziland, Zimbabwe

Rain & Weather

The rainy season is from March to November, but the western region remains dry. Winter nights can be cold.

Best Time to Visit: June – September

This region is in the Southern Hemisphere, so summer is November through April.

 Weather by Month

MONTH	GENERAL WEATHER CONDITIONS	EXTREME WEATHER WARNINGS
January		
February	Hot, Wet	
March		
April 1–15	Hot, Some Rain	
16–30	Hot Days, Cool Nights	
May		
June		VARIABLE YEAR ROUND
July	Hot Days, Cool Nights	
August		
September		
October 1–15	Hot Days, Cool Nights	
16–30	Hot, Some Rain	
November	Hot, Wet	
December		

Africa: Indian Ocean

Bassas da India, British Indian
Ocean Territory, Comoros,
Madagascar, Mauritius, Seychelles

Rain & Weather

Most rain falls from October through March. The West coast is much drier
than the East. Cyclones are possible at any time.

Best Time to Visit: Depends on your personal climatic preferences. The
months of May, October, and November have the most favorable weather
conditions. Summers are wetter and there is a risk of cyclones.

 ### Weather by Month

MONTH	GENERAL WEATHER CONDITIONS	EXTREME WEATHER WARNINGS
January		CYCLONE SEASON
February	Hot, Wet	January – March
March		
April	Hot, Humid	
May		
June 1–15	Hot, Humid	
16–30	Cooler Nights	
July	Cooler Nights	WET YEAR ROUND
August 1–15	Cooler Nights	
16–31	Hot, Humid	
September	Hot, Humid	
October		
November	Hot, Wet	
December		

Africa Packing

Africa is known for its heat. Although most of Africa is hot, there are some regions that experience cooler temperatures and colder nights as well as much rainfall. (Refer to the climate charts.) A trip to Victoria Falls for example will present you with a blanket of cool mist year round. If traveling independently in Africa (which is not recommended), it's very important for women to not dress provocatively. Provocative dress includes tank tops, short skirts, and shorts. If on a guided tour, the same guidelines exist, but women will be able to wear longer shorts more often. Don't wear a lot of jewelry or expensive clothing.

Women's Packing List

ITEM	RATIONALE
(3) pants, one convertible to shorts	Pants are preferred over shorts for cultural and hygienic reasons. One pair should convert to shorts.
(3) blouses or safari shirts, long sleeved	Keeps you cooler than having your arms exposed. Sleeves can be rolled up, or shirts can be worn unbuttoned with undershirt.
(3) camisoles/ tanks	Can be worn as undergarments to keep other shirts from being soiled with sweat.
(3) T-shirts: loose fitting, thin, ¾ sleeved	To be worn when on safari or double as sleep wear. Should wash and dry easily.
(1) skirt (below the knee)	Should match with blouses and tees. Can be worn for dressier occasions or shopping.
(1) pullover, sweater or micro-fleece jacket	Nights are sometimes cool.
(5) underwear	Should wash and dry easily. Fabric must be breathable.
(2) bras	Same as above.
(1) sleep wear	Light and comfortable, but covers skin.
(1) flip flops	For relaxing and showering. Should only be worn indoors.
(1) lightweight hiking shoes	No leather athletic shoes. Choose thinner, cooler material. Don't bring new shoes.
(4) socks: microfiber, not cotton	Cotton retains too much moisture.
(1) hat	Should provide shade and protection from blowing sand and dirt.

📦 Men's Packing List

ITEM	RATIONALE
(2) pants: cargo or your preference	You should choose the type of pants that you are most comfortable wearing often.
(1) shorts	Can be worn when pants need to be washed.
(1) nicer khaki pants	Will be clean, and worn only for dressier occasions.
(3) shirts: button down, safari style, one long sleeved	Can be worn with nice khakis or on cooler nights.
(4) T-shirts	Will be the most worn shirts.
(5) underwear	Easy wash, easy dry. Light, breathable fabric.
(4) socks: microfiber, not cotton	Cotton retains too much moisture.
(1) flip flops	For relaxing or showering.
(1) lightweight hiking shoes	No leather athletic shoes. Choose thinner, cooler material. Don't bring new shoes.
(1) sleep wear	Based on personal preference keeping in mind that nights may be cooler and there may be bugs.
(1) pullover, sweater or micro-fleece jacket	For cool nights.
(1) hat	Should provide shade and protection from blowing sand and dirt.

📦 For Men & Women — For Rain or Cooler Months Add:

ITEM	RATIONALE
Poncho or light rain jacket	If you get caught in a downpour, you will be glad you have it.
Light rain pants	If you are out on safari or touring about, they will keep you dry and clean.
Waterproof hat	Also useful in downpours.

Sports

A safari is its own sport, and the wardrobe is already designed to fit that criterion. It's unlikely you will need a swimming suit. However, if you're staying at a place with a pool or plan to swim in the ocean, bring it along.

Colors

Bright pastels and whites are not recommended. Stay with earth tones and blues. Subdued pinks and yellows are also okay.

Style

Casual/Conservative = independent traveler
Casual/Moderate = safari or group tours

Safety

Moderate to low

Tours

Since most people visit Africa on a tour, this wardrobe will suffice unless the tour operator indicates a necessary additional item.

Special Note for the Seychelles Islands

If you're planning to visit just the Seychelles, you can follow the Caribbean/South Pacific packing list, page 125. If you're planning a continental African trip and a visit to the Seychelles, you will need to use the Africa packing list, and include some items from the Caribbean/South Pacific list.

Other Notes

If you're combining a European trip with a visit to Morocco, you will need to pay close attention to the difference in culture. Some items in the European packing list, page 62, can be applied.

Be sure to pay close attention to the fabrics you choose for this region. Comfort is very important.

You will need to take all necessary clothing items with you. There is little chance of picking up forgotten articles of clothing in Africa.

Recommended Luggage

- Pullmans are not recommended. Pulling your luggage on dirt or rocky walkways is not easy.
- Small backpacks are good. Don't bring a large backpack unless you don't have to carry it. However, you don't want to burden someone else with it either.
- Duffel bags are okay, but are difficult to carry. Most adventure outfitters will require the use of a duffel bag.

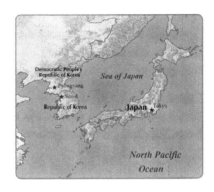

Northeast Asia

Japan, South Korea

Rain & Weather

The monsoon begins at the end of June and continues through August. It can also be rainy from March through May. It does snow in the winter. Summers are very hot and humid while winters are very cold and dry.

Best Time to Visit: April – May and September – October

If you plan to visit during the changing seasons, you will need to vary your wardrobe accordingly. A Multiple Climate pack, page 141, may be necessary.

 Weather by Month

MONTH	GENERAL WEATHER CONDITIONS	EXTREME WEATHER WARNINGS
January	Cold	WINTER
February	Cold	WINTER
March		
April 1–15	Cool	RAIN
April 16–30	Warm	RAIN
May	Warm	
June		HOT
July	Hot, Humid	MONSOON
August		MONSOON
September 1–15	Hot, Humid	
September 16–30	Warm	
October	Cool	
November 1–15	Cool	WINTER
November 16–30	Cold	WINTER
December	Cold	

China: North & Western Asia

Beijing, Harbin, Kazakhstan, Kyrgyzstan, Mongolia, Tajikistan, Tibet, Turkmenistan, Urumqi, Uzbekistan

Rain & Weather

Rain is heavy in July and August. Northern China has four distinct seasons with winters being cold and dry and summers hot and humid.

Best Time to Visit

China: October (avoid domestic holidays such as Chinese New Year); Tibet, Mongolia: July–August; Northern Kyrgyzstan: June–September; Southern Kyrgyzstan: March–October; Kazakhstan, Turkmenistan, Uzbekistan, Tajikistan: April–June and September–October; Urumqi: May–October

Careful attention to cultural concerns is necessary. Depending on your trip's itinerary, a Multiple Climate pack, page 141, may be necessary.

 Weather by Month

MONTH	GENERAL WEATHER CONDITIONS	EXTREME WEATHER WARNINGS
January–March	Cold	WINTER
April	Cool	
May	Warm	
June 1–15	Warm	
16–30	Hot, Humid	WET
July	Hot, Humid	
August		
September 1–15	Hot, Humid	
16–30	Warm	
October	Warm	
November 1–15	Cool	WINTER
16–30	Cold	
December	Cold	

Northeast Asia Packing

This region offers a rich cultural experience for the open-minded traveler. Although societies are modern, cultural tradition remains important. Attire should be conservative. Even though Japan is less conservative these days concerning restrictions about women's attire, travelers should pack conservative and classic wardrobes. It's also easy for smaller men and women to pick up cheap and decent quality clothing in Korea. It's difficult to impossible to find larger sizes.

Women's Packing List — Summer & Spring

ITEM	RATIONALE
(3) pants: one cargo or other casual, one linen drawstring or other dressier pants/ jeans are okay in spring and fall, not summer	Spring and fall are not humid, but summer is very humid. You will want cool fabrics, and you should be able to sit on the floor comfortably.
(1) shorts, longer style, (if one pants doesn't double as shorts)	Generally, you shouldn't wear shorts, but in some cases it's fine. Can double as pajamas or be worn while doing the washing.
(1) skirt	Not too short, can be slightly above the knee. Should be able to sit on the floor comfortably.
(3) tops: one long sleeved, one short	Should match with skirt, pants and shorts.
(3) camisoles/tanks	Should not be worn without a top layer. Can be worn under unbuttoned button downs.
(3) T-shirts	Can double as pajamas.
(1) light sweater	Air conditioning is very cold.
(5) underwear	Easy to wash and dry.
(2) bras	Same as above.
(1) flip flops	For relaxing and showering. Should not be worn outside unless with socks.
(1) walking shoes	No leather athletic shoes. Should be canvas or similar and easy to remove.
(4) socks	Not cotton in the summer. Cotton is okay for spring and fall.
(1) shoes, dressier (optional)	Slip on heels are nice for evenings and dining.
(1) light jacket (optional)	Recommended for spring and fall.
(1) umbrella (optional)	It can rain throughout the year. Hotels loan umbrellas, but you should have one if you aren't staying at a large hotel.

🧳 Men's Packing List — Summer & Spring

ITEM	RATIONALE
(3) pants: one convertible cargo or other casual, one nicer chino style	Nicer pants may be needed for nighttime, dining, or clubbing.
(1) shorts	Can be worn while other clothes are being washed.
(3) T-shirts	Will be worn most of the time.
(3) button downs: one long sleeved, one short	Long sleeves will be necessary in spring and fall. Short sleeves will be good in the summer.
(5) underwear	Easy to wash and dry.
(1) flip flops	For relaxing or showering.
(1) walking shoes or loafers or both	Athletic shoes are not recommended. Canvas type walking shoes are good. Loafers look nice, but may not be good for walking.
(1) light sweater, sweatshirt or other pullover	Air conditioning can be very cold.
(1) umbrella	It can rain any time. You may get one from your hotel.

🧳 Women's Packing List — Winter & Fall

ITEM	RATIONALE
(3) pants: two wool, one jeans or other casual	Winter attire tends to be more formal.
(2) thin lycra blend turtlenecks	To be worn as bottom layer.
(1) blazer	Provides extra warmth and looks good.
(1) long top coat/ (1) umbrella	Wool is best. It's very cold. Coat should fit over sweater or blazer. Umbrella is for rain or snow.
(1) soft wool sweater	Should match everything.
(1) zipper turtleneck	Can be worn alone on warmer days or under the sweater.
(2) blouses (winter styles, can be light sweaters)	Some days are a little warmer.
(1) lycra leggings	To be worn under pants in very cold conditions. Can double as pajamas.
(1) warm pajamas (optional)	Can be thin cotton sweats.

🧳 Women's Packing List — Winter & Fall (cont.)

ITEM	RATIONALE
(2) T-shirts	Can double as pajamas, and also make a good bottom layer.
(1) set gloves, hat, scarf	It's very cold in the winter.
(5) underwear	Easy to wash and dry.
(2) bras	Same as above.
(5) socks	Wool or wool blend, thin.
(1) walking shoes or boots	Should be comfortable and dry.
(1) belt	For a more finished look.

🧳 Men's Packing List — Winter & Fall

ITEM	RATIONALE
(3) pants: one wool, one jeans, one warm casual	Need both semi-dressy and casual.
(1) sweater, cardigan or other	For warmth.
(3) shirts	Your choice depending on how cold you get.
(3) T-shirts	Can double as pajamas or are good for bottom layers.
(1) turtleneck (optional)	Depends on how cold you tend to be.
(1) blazer or other light jacket	For less cold days or dressier occasions.
(1) top coat/umbrella	A coat is essential. Can be long wool or down parka. The umbrella is for rain or snow.
(5) underwear	Easy to wash and dry.
(5) socks	Light wool or synthetic.
(1) walking shoes or boots	Should be weather resistant.
(1) set gloves, hat, scarf	For colder, blustery conditions.
(1) belt	For a more finished look.
(1) warm pajamas (optional)	Depends on your preference.
(1) set lycra long underwear	For colder conditions. Can double as pajamas.

Sports

The most popular year-round sport is hiking, but skiing and golf in Korea and Japan are also popular. If you are planning a sports trip in this region, please consult Adventure Packing, page 143.

Swimsuits

Add a swimsuit if you will be staying at a large hotel. They usually have swimming pools. Typically, beaches are not popular attractions in this region.

Variable Weather

Weather conditions can change quickly. Both wardrobes are suited to be able to dress with layers or dress for warmer conditions.

Colors

Darker colors are more suitable in the winter. In spring and fall all colors are acceptable. White is not worn very often because in many parts of Asia it's the color for mourning and funeral-wear. Greens, blues, yellows, reds, and browns are best.

Style

Moderate/Moderate

Safety

High: Women should still take precautions
Moderate: Tajikistan, Turkmenistan, Urumqi, Uzbekistan

Recommended Luggage

- 22" Pullmans for spring and summer is best.
- 24"–26" Pullmans are good for fall and winter.
- Backpacks are difficult in the hot and humid summer months, but are okay.
- Duffel bags are not recommended unless for sporting equipment.

China: South & Taiwan

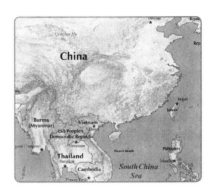

Chonqing, Guangzhou, Guiyang, Haikou, Hong Kong, Huangshi, Lanzhou, Macau, Mianyang, Nanchang, Shanghai, Taiwan, Xian, Zhengzhou

Rain & Weather

Rain is heaviest June through August. Typhoons are common along the coast. If you are traveling to the inland eastern regions or mountains, it will be significantly cooler and drier.

Best Time to Visit: March–April and October–November

A Multiple Climate pack, page 141, may be necessary depending on your itinerary.

 Weather by Month

MONTH	GENERAL WEATHER CONDITIONS	EXTREME WEATHER WARNINGS
January		
February	Warm, Dry	
March		
April	Hot, Humid	
May		
June		
July	Hot, Humid, Rainy	RAIN, TYPHOON
August		
September		
October	Hot, Humid	
November	Warm, Dry	
December		

West Asia

Bangladesh, Bhutan, Nepal,
Northern India

Rain & Weather

Monsoon rains come in June. The heaviest rain is in July and August. The East Coast has the heaviest rain. The higher elevations are substantially cooler and will require winter adventure packing (pages 143-146), particularly if you're trekking or mountain climbing. Nights can also be cold in the winter. Before the monsoon, it's very hot and dry.

Best Time to Visit: November – April

Depending on the itinerary, a Multiple Climate pack may be necessary, page 141. If you're planning to visit Bhutan or Nepal, consult Adventure Packing, pages 143–146.

 Weather by Month

MONTH	GENERAL WEATHER CONDITIONS	EXTREME WEATHER WARNINGS
January		
February	Warm, Dry	
March		
April	Hot, Dry	
May		
June		RAIN
July	Monsoon	HEAVY RAIN
August		
September		RAIN
October	Hot, Dry	
November	Warm, Dry	
December		

West Asia & South China Packing

Both India and China are slightly more conservative than other Southeast Asian destinations. China is more conservative than India. When visiting China, it's important to make an effort to blend in by choosing clothing that is not too flamboyant or extravagant. As a foreigner, you already stand out enough. In India, it's very important to adhere to dress codes when visiting shrines and temples. You will not be allowed to enter if you are wearing inappropriate clothing. Inappropriate attire includes sleeveless tops and shorts for both men and women. Women will also need to cover their heads while visiting temples.

Women's Packing List

ITEM	RATIONALE
(3) pants: loose fitting	Will be worn most of the time.
(1) shorts	Will only be worn in the hotel or as pajamas.
(1) skirt (China) or sarong (India)	Necessary for visiting temples. Should be able to double as part of a nicer ensemble for dressier situations.
(1) nicer blouse, long or ¾ sleeved	Can be worn to dress up an outfit if needed.
(2) button down blouses: long sleeved	It will be cooler with your skin covered, and you will encounter less harassment.
(3) Camisole/tanks	Can be worn as layering. A camisole under a button down provides you with the flexibility to wear the button down unbuttoned.
(4) T-shirts: ¾ sleeved or should at least provide shoulder coverage.	Useful as pajamas or on various occasions.
(1) pajamas	If you don't want to use other items as pajamas.
(1) light sweater or pullover	Air conditioning can be a problem after being in the heat.
(1) flip flops	For relaxing or showering.
(1) walking shoes	Don't take leather athletic shoes. They are too hot. Look for canvas type material.
(4) socks: microfiber, not cotton	Cotton retains too much moisture.
(5) underwear	Light fabric, easily washed, quickly dried.

🧳 Women's Packing List (cont.)

ITEM	RATIONALE
(2) bras	Same as above.
(1) hat (China), or scarf (India)	Provides shade. The scarf is useful at some temples to cover your head.

🧳 Men's Packing List

ITEM	RATIONALE
(2) pants: cargo or other travel pants	Good for travel days, etc.
(2) shorts	It's acceptable for men to wear shorts.
(4) T-shirts	Light fabric is good for every day use.
(3) button downs: two short and one long sleeved	Some situations may call for the more formal long sleeves. Short sleeve button downs are good for travel days or touring.
(1) light sweater or pullover	Air conditioning can be very cold.
(1) flip flops	For relaxing or showering.
(1) walking shoes	Don't bring leather athletic shoes. Canvas like material is better in the heat.
(4) socks: microfiber, not cotton	Keeps feet drier.
(5) underwear	Light fabric for quick dry, easy wash.
(1) hat	Shade.

🧳 Wet Season, Monsoon, Typhoon Additions

ITEM	RATIONALE
Light poncho or rain pullover and collapsible umbrella.	You may get caught in a downpour. It's best to keep yourself and your bag dry.
Make sure all your fabrics are quick drying.	If your clothes get wet, they will need to be completely dry before packing. Otherwise, they will get moldy.

Sports

This region is a trekking destination, not diving. If you are taking a trekking tour or plan to explore on your own, consult Adventure Packing, page 143.

Colors

Women in India wear bright, beautiful colors. It seems that nearly every color is acceptable except white, which indicates mourning. Black is not very popular in India, but is acceptable in China. Good colors are blues, reds, yellows, greens, and khakis.

Style

Casual/Conservative = India, Bangladesh, Bhutan, Nepal
Moderate/Moderate = South China
Dressy-Moderate/Moderate = Hong Kong

Safety

High = China
Moderate to low = other regions

Tours

If you're on a tour, the packing list is appropriate.

Other Notes

Beggars are not a problem in China. In India, however, they can be overwhelming and frustrating. Try to stay relaxed. On travel days, always wear clothing with buttoned or hidden pockets. If you are not carrying a lot of baggage, you will not get as frustrated and will more easily be able to maneuver in the crowds.

Recommended Luggage

- 22" Pullman for tours.

- Small backpacks for travelers, avoid large backpacks. You will be too heavily burdened in the crowded areas.

- Duffel bags are not recommended.

Southeast Asia 1

Cambodia, Laos, Maldives, Myanmar, Philippines, Southern India, Sri Lanka, Thailand, Vietnam

Rain & Weather

May through October is monsoon season, and rainfall can be heaviest during September and October. This region is hot and humid year round.

Best Time to Visit: November–February

Careful attention to cultural concerns is necessary.

 Weather by Month

MONTH	GENERAL WEATHER CONDITIONS	EXTREME WEATHER WARNINGS
January		
February	Hot, Humid	
March		
April		
May		
June		
July	Hot, Humid, Wet	MONSOON
August		
September		
October		
November	Hot, Humid	
December		

Southeast Asia 2

Brunei, Indonesia, Malaysia, Singapore

Rain & Weather

October through November can be the rainiest time in this region. The monsoon season is between December and March. This region is hot and humid year round.

Best Time to Visit: April–October

Indonesia note:

Papua New Guinea's climate varies slightly from the rest of Indonesia. Rainfall is not as heavy, and the east and south can be relatively dry during the December to March monsoon. Higher elevations are cooler. Papua New Guinea can be a multiple-climate pack depending on your trip's itinerary.

Careful attention to cultural concerns is necessary.

 Weather by Month

MONTH	GENERAL WEATHER CONDITIONS	EXTREME WEATHER WARNINGS
January		
February	Hot, Humid, Wet	MONSOON
March		
April		
May		
June		
July	Hot, Humid	
August		
September		
October		HEAVY RAIN
November	Hot, Humid, Wet	
December		MONSOON

Southeast Asia Packing

This area of Asia is more socially relaxed than its northern counterparts. However, there are some general wardrobe guidelines that need to be followed, especially for women. Loose pants, linen, and long sleeved blouses on travel days are best. The people are friendly and relaxed. Southeast Asians are very good salespeople. If you don't want to carry many souvenirs with you, curtail your shopping appetite until just before departure. There are plenty of opportunities to buy cheap, suitable clothing. It may be wise to take the absolute minimum wardrobe and buy items along the way.

Women's Packing List

ITEMS	RATIONALE
(1) sarong or skirt (below the knee)	Is cool and comfortable, and fits in with the culture.
(1) shorts	Usually worn by women only at the beach or other type of resort. Are useful for lounging in your room.
(3) pants: loose fitting with pockets	Could be drawstring linen or similar and/or cargo pants. Good for nights and going around town or travel days.
(3) camisole/tanks	Shouldn't be worn on their own unless at a beach or resort. Make good undergarments for wearing a button down unbuttoned.
(2) T-shirts	T-shirts can easily be replaced if they are worn out or become too soiled.
(2) blouses: ¾ sleeved, loose fitting	Are cooler than sleeveless or short sleeved because there is less direct contact with the sun.
(1) swimsuit	You never know when you might need to jump in the water because of the heat.
(1) lycra shorts, optional	Wear them under the sarong.
(5) underwear	Light fabric. Easy to wash, and quick to dry.
(2) bras	Same as above.
(1) flip flops	For relaxing or showering.
(1) walking shoes	Don't bring leather athletic shoes. It's too hot. Canvas like material is better. Don't bring new shoes.

📋 Women's Packing List (cont.)

ITEM	RATIONALE
(4) socks: microfiber, not cotton	It's hot, and cotton socks retain too much moisture. Your feet will blister.
(1) hat	Foldable Panama style provides good shade.
(1) pajamas	Necessary if you don't want to double shorts and tees as sleep wear.
(1) light sweater or pullover	Many places have air conditioning that can be shocking after being in the outdoor heat.

📋 Men's Packing List

ITEM	RATIONALE
(1) shorts	Can be worn at the beach, but not in public in Indonesia.
(3) pants: cargo or other travel type w/pockets	May be needed at night or on treks, etc.
(4) T-shirts	Will be worn on most days, and can easily be replaced.
(1) swimsuit	You may need relief from the heat.
(5) underwear	Light cotton. Easily washed and quickly dried.
(1) hat	Provides shade.
(1) flip flops	For the beach, relaxing or showering.
(2) button downs: one short sleeved, one long sleeved	Long sleeves may be needed from time to time. Short sleeved button down is good for travel days.
(1) walking shoes	Don't bring leather athletic shoes. It's too hot. Choose a canvas type material.
(4) socks: microfiber, not cotton	Cotton will retain too much moisture.
(1) light sweater or pullover	Air conditioning can be a shock after being in the heat.

Rainy Season Additions

ITEM	RATIONALE
Thin, light poncho or other pullover, and collapsible umbrella.	You may sometimes get caught in a downpour. It's nice to have something you can throw over yourself and your bag to stay dry.
Make sure everything you have packed from the packing list will dry quickly. (Check the fabric.)	If your clothes and contents of your bag do get wet, you will have to dry them completely before re-packing. Otherwise, you will have moldy clothes.

Sports
Scuba diving, snorkeling, tennis, and swimming are the most common sports. If you are planning a sports trip, you will need a small bag designated for sports equipment. If you are only bringing sports equipment *just in case,* reconsider if you aren't that enthusiastic about sports during your vacation. It's easy to rent scuba equipment if you change your mind. The extra baggage may be inconvenient, especially if it goes unused.

Colors
If you plan to do washing frequently, pastels are fine. White is not recommended since it shows dirt. Blues, yellows, reds, browns, greens and all other earth tones are best.

Style
Casual/Conservative

Safety
Moderate to low

Pajamas
If you don't want to double shorts and tees as sleep wear, you will have to add pajamas to the list.

Spa Travel
If you are going to a destination resort or for a spa trip, you can follow the Caribbean/South Pacific packing list on page 129.

Maldives
If you are going to the Maldives, you can follow the Caribbean/South Pacific pack, but keep in mind that the Maldives is an Islamic country.

Visiting Temples

You will not be allowed to enter a temple if you are wearing tank tops or shorts. Please follow the rules.

Other Notes

- Even though the weather in this region is very hot, it's advisable to wear pants and long sleeves on travel days. If you are in an air-conditioned bus or train, you will be more comfortable. If you are not in air conditioning, your skin will stay drier by not sticking to the seat.

- Especially in the cities and rural towns, women should avoid wearing shorts and tank tops. It's just not appropriate. The less skin you have exposed, the cooler you will actually be.

- Be careful drying your clothes in the sunlight, colors will fade quickly.

- Wearing loose fitting, light fabrics is the best way to keep cool. The more skin you have exposed, the hotter you will be!

Recommended Luggage

- 22" Pullman, soft or hard for destination travel.

- Small backpacks for multi-destination travel. It's too hot for large backpacks, you will be miserable with a big pack.

- Duffel bags are okay for destinations, but not for touring around. If you have to carry your bag, you will soon tire of a duffel bag.

Australia: North

Ashmore and Cartier Islands,
Coral Sea Islands, Great Barrier Reef,
N. Northern Territory,
N. Queensland, N. Western Australia

Rain & Weather

In the North and East, the monsoon comes in November and stays until March. Inland areas are relatively dry, and winters can be cool. Australia is "Down under". That means it's in the Southern Hemisphere, and the summers are from November to March. Darwin can be brutally hot year round.

Best Time to Visit: May–October

 Weather by Month

MONTH	GENERAL WEATHER CONDITIONS	EXTREME WEATHER WARNINGS
January		
February	Hot, Wet	MONSOON
March		
April	Hot	
May		
June	Medium-Hot	
July		
August		
September	Hot	
October		
November	Hot, Wet	MONSOON
December		

Australia: South

New South Wales, S. Northern
Territory, S. Queensland,
S. Western Australia, South
Australia, Tasmania, Victoria

Rain & Weather

Rain is mostly on the East Coast in the winter, March through July. It also snows in the mountains. It's typically not cold in this region. However, Tasmania can get cold.

Best Time to Visit: April–May and September–October

A Multiple Climate pack may be necessary, page 141.

 Weather by Month

MONTH	GENERAL WEATHER CONDITIONS
January	
February	Hot
March	
April	Warm
May	
June	
July	Cool
August	
September	Warm
October	
November 1–15 16–30	Warm Hot
December	Hot

New Zealand & Islands

Christmas Island; Cocos Islands; Norfolk Island; North Island, New Zealand; South Island, New Zealand

Rain & Weather

It can rain any time of year, but it rains moderately. The most precipitous time is from May through August. North Island has more moderate weather, and is pleasant year round. South Island can have cold winters, especially at higher elevations.

Best Time to Visit: Any time of the year is good.

 Weather by Month

MONTH	GENERAL WEATHER CONDITIONS
January	
February	Warm
March	
April	
May 1–15 16–31	Warm Cool
June	
July	Cool
August	
September	
October 1–15 16–31	Cool Warm
November	Warm
December	

Australia and New Zealand Packing

Australia and New Zealand are wonderful destinations with friendly and relaxed cultures. You can wear just about anything as long as it's appropriate for weather conditions.

Women's Packing List — Australia Spring & Summer

ITEM	RATIONALE
(1) light sweater	For cool nights.
(1) light blazer or jacket	For dressing up, going out, shopping.
(3) pants: drawstring with pockets or cargo	For travel days and area with bugs.
(1) skirt, length doesn't matter	For out on the town, shopping, etc.
(2) shorts	Should double as pajamas or beach wear.
(3) blouses: one long sleeved	Should match up with everything.
(3) camisole/tanks	Can be under layers or worn separately.
(3) T-shirts	Good for all purposes. Can double as pajamas or beach wear.
(1) swim suit with optional cover up	You can't go to Australia and not swim.
(5) underwear	Easy to wash and dry. Light fabric.
(2) bras	Same as above.
(1) flip flops	Will be worn a lot outside the cities. Can double as shower shoes.
(1) walking shoes	Try not to bring leather athletic shoes.
(4) socks	Don't wear your walking shoes without socks. It's too hot.
(1) dining or clubbing shoes	Slip-ons are nice and light.
(1) hat	A hat is optional, but recommended for the outback.

🧳 Men's Packing List — Australia & New Zealand — Spring & Summer

ITEM	RATIONALE
(2) pants, cargo or convertibles	For travel days or hiking in areas with bugs.
(2) shorts	Will be worn most of the time. Easy to wash.
(4) T-shirts	Good for all occasions.
(1) chinos or other dressier pants	For going out in the cities.
(2) shirts, one short sleeved, one long	Will match with the chinos for going out.
(5) underwear	Easy to wash, easy to dry. Light fabric.
(4) socks	For trekking or travel days.
(1) flip flops	For beach.
(1) walking shoes	Not leather athletic, get a breathable fabric.
(1) hat	Optional, but necessary for the outback.

🧳 Women's Packing List — Australian Winter & New Zealand Year Round

ITEM	RATIONALE
(2) pants: one convertible to shorts, one nicer	If you bring pants that can also become shorts, you don't have to pack shorts. The nicer pants are for going out in the cities.
(1) jeans	Optional. If you like jeans, this is a good destination for jeans.
(3) T-shirts, one long sleeved	The long sleeved tee will be a good layer if necessary.
(1) turtle neck	In case it gets cold or windy.
(1) light sweater	Good for nights and walks in the city when it's colder.
(1) wool sweater	In case of rain.
(1) pullover or shell jacket with a hood (waterproof)	Will function nicely in warm weather and can be worn in cold weather on top of layers.

I📷I Women's Packing List — Australian Winter/New Zealand Year Round (cont.)

ITEM	RATIONALE
(2) blouses	Can be worn with the nicer pants for going out.
(1) gloves, light	They're small and can be useful if it gets cold.
(1) pajamas	Could bring light sweats for pajamas.
(5) underwear	Comfortable and easily dried.
(2) bras	Same as above.
(1) flip flops or slippers	For relaxing.
(1) walking/hiking shoes	Leather is okay. Make sure you don't bring new shoes.
(4) socks	For walking/hiking (Could bring an extra wool pair for sleeping.)

I📷I Men's Packing List — Australian Winter/New Zealand Year Round

ITEM	RATIONALE
(2) pants: one chino, one convertible	The convertibles will be your shorts. The chinos are for going out in the cities.
(1) jeans	This is a great climate for jeans.
(2) shirts: one short sleeved, one long	Can be worn out at night or on the town.
(4) T-shirts: one long sleeved	Long sleeved shirt is for layering in the cold.
(1) light wool sweater	Good for rain.
(1) pullover or jacket shell with hood (waterproof)/ light gloves	Works well in warmer rain, and makes a good top layer in colder conditions.
(1) turtleneck	It can get cold enough for turtlenecks.
(1) flip flops	For relaxing.
(1) walking/trekking shoes	Leather is okay. Don't bring new shoes.
(4) socks	Two cotton, two light wool.
(5) underwear	Comfortable, easy wash, easy dry.

📼 Rain and Colder Conditions, June, July, August — Additions

ITEM	RATIONALE
T-shirts	Bring only one short sleeved. The others should be long sleeved.
Heavier jacket	A shell may not be enough.
Heavier sweater	Although you can purchase great wool sweaters in New Zealand, you will need at least one to wear when first arriving.
Pants	Don't necessarily need convertibles. It will probably be too cold for shorts.
(1) set hat, scarf, gloves	May be necessary.

📼 Northern Australia, Monsoon, November to February

ITEM	RATIONALE
Hooded poncho	Keeps you and your bag dry, and will not be too hot.

Sports
The above wardrobes are for touring and traveling. If you plan a sports trip, you will know what equipment you need to bring. You can pack a small sports duffel to carry your sports equipment.

Colors
There are no restrictions on colors. Be as creative as you wish. Whites are difficult to keep clean.

Style
Casual/Liberal = New Zealand and Outback Australia
Moderate/Liberal = Cities

Safety
High

Recommended Luggage
- 22" Pullman for summers are good if you will be on a tour.
- 24-26" Pullmans may be necessary for heavier winter items.
- Small backpacks are best for the independent traveler.
- Duffel bags are good for sports equipment, but remember they will have to be carried.

Europe: Continental

Austria, Belgium,
Bosnia & Herzegovina, Croatia,
Czech Republic, France,
Germany, Hungary, Liechtenstein,
Luxembourg, Moldova, Monaco,
Netherlands, Northern Italy, Poland,
Romania, Slovakia, Slovenia,
Switzerland, Yugoslavia

Rain & Weather

It can rain any time of year. Rain can be heavy in the spring, fall, and early summer. Snow can be expected in the winter.

Best Time to Visit: April–May and Mid September–Mid October

Europeans dress well. Multiple season packs may be necessary.

 Weather by Month

MONTH	GENERAL WEATHER CONDITIONS
January	Cold, Snow
February	
March	Cool
April	Warm
May	
June	Hot
July	
August	
September 1–15 16–30	Hot Warm
October 1–15 16–30	Warm Cool
November	Cool
December	Cold, Snow

Europe: Southern

Albania, Bulgaria, Greece,
Macedonia, Malta, Portugal,
Southern Italy, Spain

Rain & Weather

October through January is the rainiest time. However, rain is possible
throughout the year. Summer temperatures can be extremely hot.

Best Time to Visit: April–May and October–November

 ### Weather by Month

MONTH	GENERAL WEATHER CONDITIONS
January	Cool, Wet
February	
March	Warm, Mild
April	
May	
June	Hot, Humid
July	
August	
September	
October	Warm, Mild
November	
December	Cool, Wet

Russian Federation & Scandinavia

Denmark, Finland, Norway, Sweden, Russia

Rain & Weather

The most rain is during June, July and August. In the winter, it snows. Summers in the South can be hot. In the East, summers are rainy. In the North, summers are short. The North can have extremely harsh winters. Scandinavia is cold and dark in the winter and pleasantly warm and light in the summers.

Best Time to Visit: Mid May–Mid September

 Weather by Month

MONTH	GENERAL WEATHER CONDITIONS
January	
February	Cold
March	
April 1–15 16–30	Cold Cool
May 1–15 16–31	Cool Warm
June	
July	Warm
August	
September 1–15 16–30	Warm Cool
October	Cool
November	Cold
December	

Europe: United Kingdom

England, Ireland, Northern Ireland, Scotland, Wales

Rain & Weather

It rains throughout the year. Even though rain can be a constant, the summers can be pleasant. There are never cold or hot extremes.

Best Time to Visit: September

 Weather by Month

MONTH	GENERAL WEATHER CONDITIONS
January	
February	Cold, Wet
March	
April	Cool, Wet
May 1–15 16–31	Cool, Wet Warm, Wet
June	
July	Warm, Wet
August	
September 1–15 16–30	Warm, Wet Cool, Wet
October	Cool, Wet
November	Cold, Wet
December	

Europe Packing: East & West

A trip to Europe usually involves spending most of your time in an urban environment. There is a lot of walking, dining, visiting cafes, shopping, and touring historical and cultural sites. A more cosmopolitan style of dress is recommended in this area.

🧳 Women's Packing List — Spring & Summer

ITEM	RATIONALE
(1) black dress	For evenings or clubbing. Lycra blends are good and easy to pack.
(1) light blazer	Will dress up your entire wardrobe.
(1) skirt	Good for museums, dining, shopping, etc.
(3) pants, one dressy, two jeans or other casual	The dressier pants can be worn instead of the skirt, and the jeans can be worn on travel days or visits to the countryside.
(1) shorts	For hotter days. Style and color should match with all tops.
(3) blouses: light fabric, such as chiffon	Can be interchanged with every item.
(2) T-shirts	For more casual days.
(2) camisoles/tanks	Can create a different look using all wardrobe items.
(2) button downs, one short sleeved, one long sleeved	Short sleeves can be worn on more casual days. The long sleeves can be worn at night or on cooler days.
(1) light sweater	For nights. Should match with all other items.
(1) belt	If other items in wardrobe require a belt, bring one.
(1) pajamas	Can double as a relaxing outfit in the hotel room. Thin, light cotton sweats are good.
(5) underwear	Easy to wash and dry.
(2) bras	Same as above.
(4) socks: two pairs of stockings	The socks are for walking, and the hosiery is for dressier occasions.
(1) sandals or comfortable slip on heels	For dressier occasions.
(1) walking shoes	Preferably not athletic shoes.
(1) collapsible umbrella	It can rain at any time.
(1) light rain shell or jacket (optional)	Packs small. Can be useful.

🧳 Men's Packing List — Spring & Summer

ITEM	RATIONALE
(1) poplin jacket or other light blazer	For evenings out or museum visits.
(3) pants, one dressy, two jeans or other casual	Should match the blazer.
(1) belt	Necessary for going out on the town or other dressier occasions.
(3) button downs, two short sleeved, one long sleeved	Should match with everything. Long sleeved may be necessary at times.
(3) T-shirts	Will be worn frequently for travel days and touring the countryside.
(1) shorts	Should match with button downs and tees.
(1) light rain shell or jacket	In case of heavy rain.
(1) collapsible umbrella	It can rain at any time.
(1) loafers	For dressier occasions.
(1) walking shoes	Not athletic shoes.
(5) underwear	Easy to wash, easy to dry.
(4) socks	Should be able to be worn with loafers and with walking shoes.

🧳 Women's Packing List — Winter Europe

ITEM	RATIONALE
(3) pants, two wool, one jeans or other casual	Wool pants can be worn for dressier occasions.
(2) thin, lycra blend turtlenecks	Can easily be worn as a bottom layer without creating bulk.
(1) blazer	For dressing up pants.
(1) soft wool sweater	Should match with all items.
(1) zipper turtleneck	Can be worn on its own or under the sweater.
(3) blouses, winter (light sweaters, etc.)	Interchangeable with all items.
(2) T-shirts	Useful for layering and sleeping.
(1) top coat & umbrella	Wool, long coat. Umbrella for snow and rain.

📦 Women's Packing List — Winter Europe (cont.)

ITEM	RATIONALE
(1) lycra leggings	Can be worn as long underwear.
(1) warm pajamas	Can be a sweat suit. Some hotels are cold in the winter.
(1) set gloves, hat, scarf	It can get very cold.
(1) thick wool socks	For nights in the hotel.
(1) belt	For a more finished look.
(5) underwear	Easy to wash and dry.
(2) bras	Same as above.
(5) socks	Should be light wool.
(1) walking shoes, or boots	Be sure the shoes are comfortable and warm.

📦 Men's Packing List — Winter Europe

ITEM	RATIONALE
(3) pants, one wool, one jeans, one warm casual	Need casual and dressier attire.
(1) sweater, cardigan or other	For warmth.
(3) shirts	Your choice depending on how cold you get.
(3) T-shirts	Useful for layering and sleeping.
(1) turtleneck (optional)	Depends on how cold you tend to get.
(1) blazer	For dressier occasions.
(1) top coat & umbrella	Wool, long. Umbrella is for snow and rain.
(5) underwear	Easy to wash and dry.
(5) socks	Light wool or other synthetic.
(1) shoes or boots	Should be comfortable and appropriate with dressier attire.
(1) set gloves, scarf, hat	For colder weather and snowy conditions.
(1) belt	For a more finished look.
(1) warm pajamas	Hotels are sometimes cold in the winter.
(1) set lycra long underwear (optional)	For colder conditions.

Sports
If you're going on a sports-focused vacation, pack a sports bag. If you plan to enjoy the beaches in the summer, pack a swimming suit.

Variable Weather
Europe can be very pleasant in the spring and fall, but the weather can quickly turn cold. For unseasonably cold weather, it's easy to pick up any extra necessary clothing at your destination.

Colors
Any colors are acceptable. Light colors are best for spring and summer while darker colors are more appropriate in the winter. White should be avoided.

Style
Dressy/Liberal, Cities
Moderate/Liberal, Countryside
Moderate/Moderate = Eastern European countries

Safety
High to moderate

Recommended Luggage
- 22" to 26" Pullmans are recommended. Pullmans should easily fit through bus and train aisles.
- Backpacks are recommended for budget travelers.
- Duffel bags are not recommended because there is typically a lot of train travel, and carrying a duffle bag is inconvenient.

Additional Note
Southern Europe is not as cold in the winter. Weight of fabrics should be adjusted accordingly.

Eurasia

Armenia, Azerbaijan, Cyprus, Georgia, Turkey

Rain & Weather

The Southwest has some rain throughout the year. The inland and more easterly regions are drier and can be hotter and colder.

Best Time to Visit: April–May and October–November

 Weather by Month

MONTH	GENERAL WEATHER CONDITIONS
January	Cool
February	
March	Warm
April	
May	
June	Hot
July	
August	
September	
October	Warm
November	
December	Cool

Eastern Europe

Belarus, Estonia, Latvia,
Lithuania, Ukraine

Rain & Weather
The most rain is March through May although this region is relatively dry all year. Even though it's very hot in the summer and very cold in the winter, this region is tolerable due to its low humidity and plentiful sunshine.

Best Time to Visit: Mid-April–June and September–early October

 Weather by Month

MONTH	GENERAL WEATHER CONDITIONS
January	
February	Cold
March	
April	Warm to Cool
May	Warm
June	
July	Hot
August	
September	Warm
October	
November	Cold
December	

Eurasia/Southwest Asia/Eastern Europe Packing

This area, with the exception of Turkey, is not a popular tourist destination. However, if you are planning a trip here, it's important to note some cultural considerations when packing. Women should dress conservatively. Shorts are generally not recommended.

Women's Packing List

ITEM	RATIONALE
(3) pants: one drawstring, one convertible cargo, one jeans	Cargo pants can double as shorts to be worn only in the hotel room if it's hot.
(1) skirt	Should be below the knee, and not too tight. Wrap-around skirts are okay.
(3) button downs: long sleeved, loose fit	Can be worn over camisoles, and should match with pants and skirt.
(3) T-shirts: ¾ sleeved or loose short sleeved	Can be worn for exploring or double as pajamas.
(3) camisoles/tanks	Should not be worn on their own. Can be worn under unbuttoned button downs.
(1) light sweater	For cooler times. Should match with everything.
(1) light rain jacket, shell (optional)	The region is pretty dry, but Eurasian countries can experience some rain year round.
(5) underwear	Easy to wash and easy to dry.
(2) bras	Same as above.
(4) socks	Microfiber is best.
(1) flip flops	For relaxing or showering.
(1) walking shoes	Athletic shoes are okay, but may be too hot in some summer months. Light canvas is also good.
(1) hat or scarf to cover head	May be needed in the heat or for cultural concerns.
(1) pajamas	Light, cotton pants can combine with a T-shirt, or you may choose to bring actual pajamas.

Men's Packing List

ITEM	RATIONALE
(3) pants: cargo or other casual, one chino	One pair can be convertible to shorts and worn when appropriate.
(3) button downs: one short sleeved, one long	Should match with pants.
(4) T-shirts	Will be worn most of the time. Can double as pajamas.
(1) light sweater or sweatshirt	For cooler times.
(1) hat (optional)	Can provide shade on hot days.
(5) underwear	Easy to wash, easy to dry.
(4) socks	Microfiber is best.
(1) flip flops	For relaxing or showering.
(1) walking shoes	Athletic shoes are okay. Canvas may be better. Depends on your preference.

Winter & Higher Elevations — Additions

ITEM	RATIONALE
(1) set hat, gloves, scarf	It can be snowy and windy in the winter.
(1) wool sweater, medium-heavy weight	Should match with everything.
(1) shell jacket	To be worn as top layer to protect against the elements.
Pants should be heavier weight.	Wool or other heavier fabric.
(1) set long underwear	Should be thin, microfibers are best.
(2) turtlenecks	Provide extra warmth when necessary.
Shoes should be of waterproof fabric.	For walking in snow and rain.
Button downs can be replaced with winter style shirts.	For added warmth.

Sports

If you are going to this area on a sports trip, please consult Adventure Packing, page 143.

Colors

Colors shouldn't be too bright. You will attract less attention if you wear earth tones. Black should be avoided, but is okay at night. Don't take white.

Style

Casual/Conservative

Safety

Moderate to low

Cultural Concerns

Women should be cautious and conservative. Don't wear sleeveless blouses in public, and shorts are generally unacceptable. You will not be hot in the summer if you choose light and loose pants. Men have fewer restrictions, but generally should follow local rules.

Recommended Luggage

- 22" Pullmans are good for city trips.

- Small backpacks are best if you're planning a lot of overland travel.

- Duffel bags are not recommended.

Middle East 1

Afghanistan, Kuwait, Iran, Iraq, Pakistan

Rain & Weather

From July to September, there is a monsoon in the eastern region; however, the western region is dry at this time. Higher elevations, including mountains, can experience harsh winters. Be aware that the sun's rays are excessively strong, so covering your arms and legs is not only culturally responsible, but physically healthy. Wear sunglasses, or bring a hat to protect your eyes and forehead from the sun.

Best Time to Visit: April–May and September–October

A Multiple Climate pack, page 141, may be necessary. Cultural considerations are very important in this region.

 Weather by Month

MONTH	GENERAL WEATHER CONDITIONS
January	Cool
February	
March	Warm, Dry
April	
May	Hot, Dry
June	
July	
August	
September	
October	Warm, Dry
November	
December	Cool

Middle East 2

Bahrain, Oman, Qatar, Saudi Arabia,
United Arab Emirates, Yemen

Rain & Weather

From April until October, this region is usually hot and dry but humid along the coast. From December to January, winter rain occurs as one or two heavy storms. Otherwise, there is little rain. Winter days usually begin as cool then become warm, with sunset relieving the heat. Late evening may be cool or occasionally chilly causing frost or light snow in the mountain areas. Summers are excessively hot and uncomfortable. Two exceptions: Al Ain in the UAE enjoys spring-like weather conditions from November to March; and Salalah in southern Oman has constant monsoon rains, the Khareef, from late June until late August, turning the surrounding mountains and desert green.

Best Time to Visit: November–March

Attention to cultural differences is extremely important in this region, especially during Ramadan. The more conservative you dress the better. However, men are advised not to bring ties. They are only worn for special, state visits. In Saudi Arabia only, all women are now required to wear an abaya, a silk cloth that covers the shoulders to the feet. Veils covering the hair and neck may be necessary during holy days. Buy one there. Local men and women in the Gulf also cover their bodies to protect them from the sun. Smart tourists do the same.

 Weather by Month

MONTH	GENERAL WEATHER CONDITIONS	MONTH	GENERAL WEATHER CONDITIONS
January	Warm, chilly nights	July	Excessively Hot, Dry but Humid along coast
February	Warm, cool nights	August	
March		September	
April	Hot, Dry	October	Warm, cool nights
May	Excessively Hot, Dry but Humid along coast	November	
June		December	Warm, chilly nights

Middle East 3

Israel, Jordan, Lebanon, Syria

Rain & Weather

From November to February, some rain can be expected along the Mediterranean coast. Inland areas stay pretty dry, and are drier and warmer year round.

Best Time to Visit: April–May and October–November

Cultural considerations are important in this area.

 ## Weather by Month

MONTH	GENERAL WEATHER CONDITIONS
January	Cool
February	Mild, Some Rain
March	
April	
May	Hot, Dry
June	
July	
August	
September	
October	Warm, Dry
November	Mild, Some Rain
December	

Middle East Packing

This is an often-overlooked destination that has a lot to offer visually and culturally. Aside from the obvious areas that cannot easily be visited, there is beauty and mystique to be found in this region. Cultural considerations are important in most of the countries, but Israel has more relaxed rules concerning attire. Since Israel is the most popular destination in this area, the lists are more focused on Israel, however, items that can be worn throughout the region are included.

It's important to note that in some of the more conservative Arab countries, you cannot enter if you have an Israeli visa or stamp in your passport. You can schedule your visit to Israel after visiting other Arab countries, or ask the Israeli Consulate or Embassy where you get your visa to put it on a separate piece of paper that can be stapled (and later removed) from your passport.

Women's Packing List

ITEM	RATIONALE
(1) solid colored dress (should be a conservative style for Muslim countries)	Should be ankle length for Muslim countries. Can be slightly shorter in Israel.
(1) skirt (way below the knee)	Length depends on destination. (Longer for Arabian countries.) Should be light and flowing, not denim or other stiff fabric.
(3) blouses: nice, long or ¾ sleeved	Should match with pants, skirt and dress. Can be worn as a cover with the dress or used to dress up pants.
(3) pants: one cargo, two other (drawstring, loose, etc.) Avoid tight pants. It's usually too hot for jeans.	Useful for hiking, touring, etc. The other pants are good for shopping, and city touring.
(1) shorts	Can double as pajamas or worn when doing laundry, or while relaxing—not in public.
(3) camisole/tanks	Typically should not be worn without a blouse on top. Doubles as pajamas on hot nights. Provides a layer of warmth for cool nights.
(3) T-shirts	Can be worn in a variety of situations, but short sleeves should not be worn in Arabian countries. ¾ sleeves are best.
(1) light pullover or sweater/ jacket/blazer	For cool nights or dressier occasions.

📷 Women's Packing List (cont.)

ITEM	RATIONALE
(5) underwear	Easily washed and dried, cool fabric.
(2) bras	Same as above.
(1) flip flops	For relaxing or showering.
(1) walking shoes	No leather athletic shoes. Canvas type material is better. Don't take new shoes. Sandals are worn by most people.
(4) socks, microfiber not cotton	Cotton retains too much moisture.
(1) hat or scarf	Multiple uses.

📷 Men's Packing List

ITEM	RATIONALE
(1) shorts (rarely worn in public by men)	Men will want to wear pants more often in Arabian countries.
(3) pants, two cargo or other style depending on personal preference, one chinos	The chinos are for dressier occasions and will be useful in Arabian countries
(3) shirts, two short sleeved, one long sleeved	Can be worn with chinos for dressier times. More appropriate than T-shirts in Arabian countries.
(4) T-shirts	Good for everyday in Israel, and on occasion in Arabian countries.
(5) underwear	Easily washed and dried. Light fabric.
(4) socks, microfiber not cotton	Cotton retains too much moisture.
(1) flip flops	Good for relaxing and showering.
(1) walking/hiking shoes	No leather athletic shoes. Canvas type material is better. Don't take new shoes.
(1) poplin jacket or light pullover/sweater	The poplin jacket is good for more formal situations in Arabian countries. The pullover is good for cool nights in Israel.
(1) hat	Baseball caps are now considered appropriate in Arabic countries. You may also choose another style according to your preference.

Rain or Monsoon Additions

ITEM	RATIONALE
Light Rain Jacket	Can layer other clothing from list underneath for cool rain, or wear over a T-shirt for warm rain.
Umbrella	May be necessary in the winter in Israel.
Warmer sweater/ and fabric choices	For winters in Israel.

Sports
If you plan to participate in sports, you can pack a light sports duffel. If you plan to swim, add a swimsuit to the list.

Colors
Dark colors are okay in this region, but may make you hot. Bright colors and pastels are fine in Israel but inappropriate in Arabian nations. White is okay, but easily shows the dirt. Earth tones are always a good choice. Blues are also good.

Style
Moderate/Conservative, countryside and Israel
Dressy/Conservative, cities

Safety
Moderate to low

Tours
You may be able to dress slightly less conservatively on a tour in Arabian countries, but following the list is still a good idea. If you are not on a tour, many five-star hotels offer day trips or overnight trips.

Other Notes
- Don't call unnecessary attention to yourself by wearing lots of jewelry or dressing in lavish clothing.
- Respect the cultural guidelines of the countries. Don't impose your personal preferences.

Recommended Luggage
- 22" Pullmans are best in this region if you don't have to do excessive traveling and moving.
- Small backpacks are okay. Large backpacks should be avoided.
- Duffel bags are okay if you don't mind carrying them.

North America: Canada, Southern Ontario

Southern Ontario

Rain & Snow

The North can have extreme winters with much snow. Otherwise, precipitation is moderate. There are four seasons in this region.

Best Time to Visit: June–October

A Multiple Climate pack, page 141, may be necessary.

 Weather by Month

MONTH	GENERAL WEATHER CONDITIONS
January	
February	Cold
March	
April	Cool
May	Warm
June	
July	Warmest
August	
September	Warm
October	Cool
November	
December	Cold

North America: Eastern Canada

New Brunswick, Newfoundland, Nova Scotia, Prince Edward Island, Quebec

Rain & Snow

There can be heavy snow in the winter and rain in the summers. There is more precipitation in the East.

Best Time to Visit: June–August

A Multiple Climate pack, page 141, may be necessary.

 Weather by Month

MONTH	GENERAL WEATHER CONDITIONS
January	
February	Cold
March	
April	Cool
May	Warm
June	
July	Warmest
August	
September	Warm
October	Cool
November	
December	Cold

North America: Canada, Southern Ontario & Eastern Canada Packing

Except for in cities like Toronto, Canada is very casual. There are no cultural restrictions concerning attire. The weather, however, requires attention. It can be warm in the summer months, but not as warm as in other North American regions. People are generally kind and accepting, so there is no need to worry about fitting in. Many Americans think once they cross the US/Canadian border, the weather is Arctic. This is especially untrue for the areas closest to the US border. Parkas are not necessary in the summer, unless you plan to go very far north.

Women's Packing List — Spring & Summer

ITEM	RATIONALE
(3) pants, one slightly dressier, jeans are okay	For traveling around or for sightseeing in the cities.
(1) shorts	Some days will require shorts, but you may find pants more practical for most days and nights.
(1) skirt	Not too dressy. You will be able to dress nicer for nights out, or museum trips.
(3) T-shirts, one long sleeved	You may need the long sleeves if it gets cooler.
(3) blouses, one long sleeved, two short	Should match with pants, shorts, and skirt.
(3) camisoles	Can be worn alone or under blouses.
(1) light to medium sweater (wool is okay)	May be necessary at night or even some days.
(1) pajamas	A comfortable, but light sweat suit is good for sleeping and comes in handy.
(1) jacket or wind breaker	Can be worn as a top layer if it rains or if you go to higher elevation.
(1) walking shoes	Athletic shoes are okay. Short, canvas boots are also good for all around use.
(1) flip flops	For relaxing or showering.
(1) nicer shoes (optional)	For going out or dressier occasions.
(5) underwear	Easy to wash and dry.
(2) bras	Same as above.
(4) socks	Cotton is okay.
(1) hat (optional)	For bad hair days. The sun is not too much of a problem.

🧳 Men's Packing List — Spring & Summer

ITEM	RATIONALE
(3) pants, one casual, one dressier, jeans are okay	You may want to dress nicer in the evenings.
(1) shorts	You only need one here because it's easy to do laundry. You can wear shorts while wearing the pants and vice versa.
(4) T-shirts, one long sleeved	The long sleeved shirt is for cooler nights.
(2) button downs, one short sleeved, one long	Should match with pants and shorts.
(1) pullover, sweater or sweatshirt	For cooler days and nights.
(1) light shell jacket	In case of rain or cold.
(1) pajamas	Can use other items to double, but your clothes will stay cleaner if you bring sleep wear.
(1) walking shoes	Athletic shoes are okay. Canvas hikers are also good.
(1) flip flops	For relaxing or showering.
(5) underwear	Easy to wash and dry.
(4) socks	Cotton is okay.

🧳 Women's Winter Packing

ITEM	RATIONALE
(3) pants, two wool, one jeans or other casual	Pants should be large enough to wear over long underwear if necessary.
(1) set long underwear	Microfiber is best. Can double as pajamas.
(3) turtlenecks or warm undershirts	Will be needed as part of a layering system. Can double as pajamas.
(2) T-shirts	Good first layering if it's too warm for long underwear.
(2) winter blouses	Should match with everything.
(1) soft wool sweater	Medium to heavy weight is recommended.
(1) winter coat, parka or other warm top coat	Will be worn most of the time.
(1) short or high boots good for rain and snow	Will keep your feet warmer than shoes.

🧳 Women's Winter Packing (cont.)

ITEM	RATIONALE
(1) shoes, other	For dressier occasions or warmer days.
(4) socks	Wool.
(1) thick wool socks or slippers	Can be worn while sleeping on cold nights.
(1) sweatpants or other warm pajama pants (optional)	Can be worn with a turtleneck or T-shirt.
(5) underwear	Easy to wash and dry.
(2) bras	Same as above.
(1) set hat, scarf, gloves	Very necessary when it's windy or snowy.
(1) belt (if styles chosen require it)	Looks nicer.

🧳 Men's Winter Packing

ITEM	RATIONALE
(3) pants, one wool, one jeans, one warm and casual	Need to have one nicer pair of pants.
(1) sweater, wool	Will be necessary as part of layering.
(3) turtlenecks or other warm undershirt	For everyday use.
(3) T-shirts	Can provide an extra layer or double as pajamas.
(1) coat, parka or other winter coat	For top layer.
(1) set gloves, hat, scarf	Will sometimes be necessary.
(4) socks	Wool
(1) hiking boots or other weather boots	For walking through snow, rain, etc.
(1) other shoes (optional)	May choose loafers for dressier times.
(5) underwear	Easy to wash, easy to dry.
(1) warm pajamas (optional)	If not using T-shirts or long underwear for sleeping.
(1) set long underwear	May be necessary on colder days and nights.

Sports

If you will be swimming in the summer, add a swimsuit. If you are planning to ski in the winter, prepare an extra ski bag.

Colors

Generally, all colors are acceptable. It's not advisable to travel with white, however. It's much too difficult to keep clean. Darker colors are good all around colors in Canada since it's never too hot. Bright colors are okay in the summer and spring, but make sure everything matches.

Style

Casual/Liberal

Safety

High

Variable Weather

Like any other Continental climate, the weather can change quickly. Umbrellas are not included in the lists. It's easy to purchase an umbrella if you don't want to pack one.

Recommended Luggage

- 22"-26" Pullmans are good.
- Small backpacks work well if you're planning a lot of outdoor activities.

North America: Pacific Northwest

Northern California, Oregon, Washington, British Columbia

Rain & Weather

Rain is year round. Summers, however, can be dry at times.

Best Time to Visit: May-October

A Multiple Climate pack, page 141, may be necessary.

 Weather by Month

MONTH	GENERAL WEATHER CONDITIONS
January	
February	Cold, Rain
March	
April	
May	Warm, Rain
June	
July	
August	Warmer, Some Rain
September	
October	
November	Cool, Rain
December	

North America: Pacific Northwest Packing

This region is beautiful and very green, caused from a lot of rain! You should not ignore the importance of rain gear in this area. Culturally, there are no restrictions for attire. However, you may not want to bring short skirts and short shorts due to the probability of rain.

Women's Packing List

ITEM	RATIONALE
(3) pants, one casual, one cooler and dressier, jeans are okay	You will want a nicer pair of pants for going out.
(1) shorts	Can be worn most summer days.
(1) skirt	For dressier occasions.
(1) dress, black	For clubbing.
(1) blazer (good in San Francisco) optional	Will give your wardrobe a dressier look.
(3) blouses	Should match with shorts, skirt, and pants.
(3) camisoles	Can be worn alone on hot days, or under blouses for a dressier look.
(3) T-shirts, one long sleeved	Can be useful for layering on wet days.
(1) jacket/pullover/or other rain protections	Necessary.
(1) Umbrella	Necessary.
(1) sweater, light to medium weight	Nights can be much cooler. Should be nice enough to wear with the skirt if necessary.
(1) pajamas (optional) can be light sweats	If not using shorts and tees to double as pajamas.
(5) underwear	Easy to wash and dry.
(2) bras	Same as above.
(4) socks, (2) nylons	Light fabric.
(1) short boots or other walking shoes	To protect from moisture.
(1) shoes, nicer heels	For going out or dining.
(1) flip flops	For relaxing or showering.
(1) hat (optional)	May be necessary in the rain.

📦 Men's Packing List

ITEM	RATIONALE
(3) pants, one casual, one dressier	Dressier pants are for going out.
(1) shorts	Some days may be hot.
(3) T-shirts, one long sleeved	Long sleeves are for cooler times.
(2) button downs, one short sleeved, one long	Long sleeves are better for nights.
(1) light sweater, or pullover	In case layering is necessary.
(1) rain jacket and/or (1) blazer	For rain.
(1) walking shoes or short boots	Good for all around wear.
(1) dressier shoe, loafer (optional)	Good for going out.
(1) flip flops	For relaxing or showering.
(1) umbrella	Necessary.
(5) underwear	Easy to wash and dry.
(4) socks	Light fabric
(1) hat (optional)	May be necessary in the rain.

📦 Winter Alterations

ITEM	RATIONALE
Take out shorts, add another pair of pants	You will not need shorts.
Choose heavier fabrics and winter styles.	Follow the packing list, but take winter styles and fabrics.
Take out one T-shirt, and add a turtleneck.	It's not really cold, but much cooler in the winter.
Bring long sleeves instead of short except for two T-shirts.	You will need the warmth.
(2) sweaters	Since you will be wearing them more often, you may want to bring two.
Warmer shoes	For obvious reasons.

Sports

If you plan to swim, bring a swimsuit. Hiking, climbing, biking and kayaking are popular in this region. You may also need to pack a sports bag.

Colors

Black is a popular color in this region. It's fine for day and night. Any colors are appropriate as long as they match. White is never good for traveling.

Style

Casual/Liberal
Moderate-Dressy/Liberal = San Francisco

Safety

High to moderate

Recommended Luggage

- 22"–24" Hard-side Pullmans are recommended since it's likely your bag will get wet.

- Backpacks can be difficult due to rainfall, but recommended for adventures.

- Duffel bags are fine for sports gear.

United States: Rocky Mountains & Northern Mountains

Colorado, Idaho, Montana, New Mexico, Utah, Wyoming

Rain & Weather

Rain showers are possible throughout the summer months. Summer days can be hot while summer nights can get cold. Lower elevations are much more temperate. Snow is possible at higher elevations from October through June. However, most of the snow is in the winter months. This region can have hot days and cold nights. Temperatures can change quickly. The region has overall low humidity.

Best Time to Visit: Mid April–May and Mid September–Mid October

A Multiple Climate pack, page 141, is recommended.

 Weather by Month

MONTH	GENERAL WEATHER CONDITIONS
January	
February	Cold
March	
April	1–15: Cool 16–30: Warm
May	Warm
June	1–15: Warm 16–30: Hot
July	
August	Hot
September	1–15: Hot 16–30: Warm
October	1–15: Warm 16–30: Cool
November	
December	Cold

United States: Midwest & Mid North

Illinois, Iowa, Kansas, Michigan, Minnesota, Missouri, Nebraska, North Dakota, South Dakota, Wisconsin

Rain & Weather

The least precipitation is in January and February. Rain is possible throughout the year. Snowstorms in the winter can be treacherous. Winters are extremely cold, and summers are very hot and humid. Tornadoes hit the southern region in late spring.

Best Time to Visit: September–October

 ### Weather by Month

MONTH	GENERAL WEATHER CONDITIONS
January	
February	Cold
March	
April	Cool, Warm
May	
June	
July	Hot, Humid
August	
September	Cool, Warm
October	
November	Cold
December	

U.S.: Rocky Mountains, Midwest, North Packing

This region is characterized by extremes in weather. No matter what the season in the Rocky Mountains or the northern states, a sweater or jacket is always necessary. The Midwest has the hottest and most humid summers.

There are no cultural restrictions concerning attire, but the general mode of dress is less cosmopolitan than areas like New York and Los Angeles.

Women's Packing List — Spring & Summer

ITEM	RATIONALE
(3) pants: one casual (jeans are okay), one dressier	You will need something for the countryside and something for the cities.
(2) shorts or skirts	It can get very hot in the summer.
(1) skirt	Should be casual yet elegant. Good for going out on the town.
(3) T-shirts	Good for all purposes. Can also double as pajamas.
(2) camisoles/tanks	Can be worn alone or as a bottom layer.
(2) blouses: one long sleeved, one short	Even hot summer days can have cool nights. Long sleeves are also necessary in the mountains where there are many mosquitoes.
(1) sweater, light to medium weight	Spring and fall can be quite cold. Summers can also turn cold instantly in the mountains.
(1) light jacket/pullover/ or blazer	Same as above.
(1) pajamas (optional)	If T-shirts are not doubling for pajamas.
(5) underwear	Easy to wash and dry.
(2) bras	Same as above.
(4) socks	Cotton is okay.
(1) flip flops (optional)	For relaxing or showering.
(1) walking/hiking shoes	Good hiking boots will be necessary for outdoor activities. Don't bring new shoes. Athletic shoes are not good for hiking.
(1) shoes, dressier	For wearing with skirt and nicer pants.
(1) hat (optional)	For bad hair days or protection from the sun.

Men's Packing List — Spring & Summer

ITEM	RATIONALE
(3) pants: one casual (jeans are okay), one dressier	You will want dressier pants for city activities. Pants will be worn more in the spring and fall.
(2) shorts	Will be worn on most summer days.
(3) T-shirts	Can double as pajamas. Will be worn most days.
(2) button downs: one long sleeved, one short	Nights can get cool.
(1) sweater or other heavier shirt	In case you need a warm top layer.
(1) jacket/pullover/or blazer	For dressier times or rainy conditions.
(5) underwear	Easy to wash and dry.
(4) socks	Cotton is okay.
(1) pajamas (optional)	It's up to you.
(1) walking or hiking shoes	Necessary for outdoor activities. Athletic shoes are not as good for hiking in the mountains.
(1) flip flops (optional)	For relaxing or showering.
(1) loafers or other dressier shoes	For going out.
(1) hat (optional)	For bad hair days or sun protection.

Women's Winter Packing

ITEM	RATIONALE
(3) pants: one wool, two jeans or other casual	Because it's often too cold for skirts, nicer pants are required to replace skirts.
(1) blazer	For dressier occasions.
(2) sweaters, medium to heavy	To keep warm.
(2) turtlenecks	For layering.
(1) set long underwear (optional)	If you will be outside a lot in the winter.
(1) set hat, gloves, scarf	Necessary most of the winter.
(2) winter blouses	Need to match pants and sweaters.

🧳 Women's Winter Packing (cont.)

ITEM	RATIONALE
(1) winter coat	Style depends on your trip's itinerary.
(4) socks	Thin wool is best.
(1) boots or other protective shoes	Should be waterproof or leather.
(1) slippers or thick socks	For relaxing at night.
(1) sweat suit or pajamas	Should be comfortable and warm.
(5) underwear	Easy to wash and dry.
(2) bras	Same as above.
(1) belt	For a more finished look.

🧳 Men's Winter Packing

ITEM	RATIONALE
(3) pants: one wool, one jeans, one warm and casual	Will need to have at least one pair of nicer pants.
(1) sweater, wool	Provides a good top layer.
(3) turtlenecks or other warm undershirts.	For everyday use.
(3) T-shirts	Can provide an extra layer or double as pajamas.
(1) blazer	For dressier occasions.
(2) button downs, long sleeved	One dressier, one can be flannel for more casual dress.
(1) winter coat	Style depends on your plans.
(1) set hat, gloves, scarf	Higher elevations will require it.
(5) underwear	Easy to wash and dry.
(4) socks	Thin wool is best.
(1) boots/shoes	Should protect against moisture.
(1) shoes, dressier	For cities.
(1) set long underwear (optional)	Necessary for outdoor activities.

Sports

Snow skiing, rafting, horseback riding, mountain climbing, cycling, swimming, tennis, golf, and water skiing are all possible activities in this area. If you are planning a sports trip, pack a sports bag.

Colors

All colors are acceptable. White is not recommended.

Style

Casual/Liberal
Moderate/Liberal = Cities

Safety

High to moderate

Variable Weather

It's very important to note that weather conditions can change rapidly.

Recommended Luggage

- 22" – 26" Pullmans are best for city trips.
- Backpacks are necessary for camping trips.
- Rolling duffel bags are good for ski gear and other sports equipment.

United States: East

Delaware, Indiana, Kentucky, Maryland, New Jersey, Ohio, Pennsylvania, Virginia, Washington D.C., West Virginia

Rain & Weather

Rain is possible throughout the year. It snows in the winter months. Summers are hot and humid while winters can be very cold.

Best Time to Visit: April–May and mid September–October

 Weather by Month

MONTH	GENERAL WEATHER CONDITIONS
January	
February	Cold, Wet
March	
April	Drier, Warm
May	
June	
July	Hot, Humid
August	
September 1–15	Hot, Humid
16–30	Drier, Warm
October	Drier, Warm
November 1–15	Drier, Warm
16–30	Cold, Wet
December	Cold, Wet

United States: Northeast

Connecticut, Maine, Massachusetts, New Hampshire, New York, Rhode Island, Vermont

Rain & Weather

Rain is steady throughout the year. Winter storms can be bad. Summers are hot and humid. Inland winters are snowy and cold. Higher elevations are cooler.

Best Time to Visit: April–May and mid September–October

A Multiple Climate pack, page 141, may be necessary.

 Weather by Month

MONTH	GENERAL WEATHER CONDITIONS
January	
February	Cold
March	
April	Warm
May	
June	
July	Hot, Humid
August	
September 1–15	Hot, Humid
16–30	Warm
October 1–15	Warm
16–31	Cool
November 1–15	Cool
16–30	Cold
December	Cold

United States: Northeast, East Packing

This region is generally a more formal and preppy area than the West or South. Cosmopolitan attire is necessary in Eastern cities. You will fit in better if you dress up a little in the cities. Shorts and athletic shoes are not really appropriate here. There are no cultural restrictions concerning sleeve or skirt lengths. Sticking to classic styles is best.

Women's Packing List — Spring & Summer

ITEM	RATIONALE
(1) black dress	For evenings or clubbing.
(1) light blazer	To dress up your wardrobe.
(1) skirt	Good for museums and other cultural activities.
(3) pants: one dressy, two casual	Jeans can be worn on travel days or visits to the countryside.
(1) shorts	For hotter days. Styles and colors should match all tops.
(3) blouses	Should match with pants, skirt and shorts.
(3) T-shirts	Can double as pajamas or be worn alone.
(2) camisoles/tanks	Can be worn alone or with other blouses to create a different look.
(1) long sleeved button down	For cooler nights and casual circumstances.
(1) light sweater	For nights. Should match everything.
(1) belt	For a more finished look.
(1) pajamas (optional)	Can double as a relaxing outfit.
(5) underwear	Easy to wash and dry.
(2) bras	Same as above.
(4) socks/(2) pairs of nylons	Socks are for walking, hosiery is for dressier occasions.
(1) sandals or comfortable slip on heels	For dressier occasions.
(1) walking shoes	Athletic shoes are not really appropriate.
(1) umbrella (optional)	You may get caught in the rain, but your hotel will also provide umbrellas.

Men's Packing List — Spring & Summer

ITEM	RATIONALE
(1) poplin jacket or other light blazer	For evenings or cultural activities.
(3) pants: one dressy, two jeans or other casual	Should match blazer.
(1) belt	For a more finished look.
(2) shorts	Should match with all shirts.
(3) button downs: two short sleeved, one long	Long sleeved shirt is for dressier and cooler times.
(3) T-shirts	For every day wear.
(1) light sweater or shell jacket (optional)	Depends on your preference.
(1) loafers or other nicer shoes	For going out and nicer occasions.
(1) walking shoes	Athletic shoes are not recommended.
(5) underwear	Easy to wash and dry.
(4) socks	Cotton is okay.
(1) umbrella (optional)	In case of rain.

Women's Winter Packing

ITEM	RATIONALE
(3) pants: two wool, one jeans or other casual	Wool pants can be worn for dressy or casual.
(2) thin, lycra blend turtlenecks	For first layer. Can double as pajamas.
(1) blazer	For dressing up pants.
(1) soft wool sweater	Should match everything.
(1) zipper turtleneck	Can be worn alone or under sweater.
(3) blouses, winter	Should be interchangeable with all items.
(3) T-shirts	Useful for layering and sleeping.
(1) top coat	Should be warm yet fashionable.
(1) lycra leggings	In case it's really cold. Can be worn under pants.
(1) pajamas	If not doubling other items.

🧳 Women's Winter Packing (cont.)

ITEM	RATIONALE
(1) set gloves, hat, scarf	It can get really cold.
(1) thick wool socks (optional)	For nights in the hotel room.
(1) belt	For a more finished look.
(5) underwear	Easy to wash and dry.
(2) bras	Same as above.
(5) socks	Thin wool is best.
(1) shoes, short or tall boots or other walking shoes that protects from moisture	You want fashion and function.

🧳 Men's Winter Packing

ITEM	RATIONALE
(3) pants: one wool, one jeans, one warm casual	It's nice to have a variety and be prepared for dressier occasions.
(1) sweater	For warmth.
(3) shirts	Your choice depending on how cold you get.
(3) T-shirts	Useful for layering and sleeping.
(1) turtleneck (optional)	Depends on how cold you tend to get.
(1) blazer	For dressier occasions.
(1) top coat	Style will depend on plans.
(1) set gloves, hat, scarf	May be necessary in storms.
(1) pajamas (optional)	Personal preference.
(1) belt	For a more finished look.
(1) set long underwear (optional)	Personal preference.
(5) underwear	Easy to wash and dry.
(5) socks	Thin wool is best.
(1) shoes or boots	Should be comfortable and appropriate with dressier attire.

Sports
Many sports are popular in this region. If you are planning a sports trip, pack a sports bag.

Humidity
Please note that summer fabrics should be chosen for comfort in humidity.

Colors
Blacks and blues are good in the cities. Any colors are fine except for white. Spring and fall colors can be chosen according to seasonal fashion.

Style
Moderate/Liberal
Dressy/Liberal = Cities

Safety
High to moderate

Recommended Luggage
- 22"–26" Pullmans are best.
- Backpacks are generally more uncomfortable.
- Duffel bags are good for sports equipment.

United States: Southwest

Southern California, Arizona, New Mexico, Nevada

Rain & Weather

This region is fairly dry although it can rain in Southern California from October to March. Desert temperatures can get low at night in the winters. California can be very cloudy in June with higher than usual humidity. Winter nights on the coast can also be cold. Summers can be hot both in the desert and on the coast.

Best Time to Visit: March–May

 Weather by Month

MONTH	GENERAL WEATHER CONDITIONS
January	Cool, Warm
February	
March	Warm
April	
May	
June 1–15 16–30	Warm Hot
July	Hot
August	
September	
October	Warm
November	
December	Cool, Warm

United States: South

Alabama, Arkansas, Louisiana, Mississippi, Oklahoma, Tennessee, Texas

Rain & Weather

The most rain falls from December to February. Thunderstorms are possible in the summer. Tornadoes are possible in the spring, and hurricanes are possible in the summer. Heat and humidity can be intense in the summer.

Best Time to Visit: May and October–November

 Weather by Month

MONTH	GENERAL WEATHER CONDITIONS	EXTREME WEATHER WARNINGS
January	Warm, Cool	
February		
March	Warmer, Cool	TORNADOES
April		
May		
June	Hot, Humid	HURRICANES
July		
August		
September 1–15 16–30	Hot, Humid Drier, Warm	
October	Warmer, Cool	
November 1–15 16–30	Warmer, Cool Warm, Cool	
December	Warm, Cool	

United States: Southeast

Georgia, Florida, North Carolina, South Carolina

Rain & Weather

Hurricane season is from June through November. Otherwise, rain is more frequent from November to March. Southern Florida is much hotter than the northern part of the region.

Best Time to Visit: North Carolina, South Carolina, Georgia: April–May and September–October; Florida: December–May

 Weather by Month

MONTH	GENERAL WEATHER CONDITIONS	EXTREME WEATHER WARNINGS
January	Cool	
February		
March	Warm	
April		
May		
June	Hot, Humid	HURRICANES
July		
August		
September		
October	Warm	
November		
December 1–15	Warm	
16–31	Cool	

United States: Southwest, South, Southeast Packing

The southern regions are mostly casual except for Los Angeles, Miami, Atlanta, and Houston. In these major cities, styles are more cosmopolitan and trendy. There are no cultural restrictions, and people are generally kind.

🧳 Women's Packing List — Spring & Summer

ITEM	RATIONALE
(3) pants: one drawstring or other slightly dressy, two jeans or other casual	Can be dressed up or down.
(1) skirt	Should match with all tops.
(1) dress (for LA, Miami, Atlanta, Houston)	For nights out.
(2) shorts or other skirts	Should match with all tops.
(1) light blazer	To dress up wardrobe.
(2) button downs: one long sleeved	Evenings can be cool.
(2) blouses	According to current fashion.
(3) T-shirts	For all occasions.
(3) camisoles/tanks	Can be worn alone or under blouses.
(1) light sweater	For cooler times.
(5) underwear	Easy to wash and dry.
(2) bras	Same as above.
(3) socks/(1) hosiery	Cotton is okay. Hosiery for dress and skirt.
(1) flip flops or other sandals	For relaxing or showering.
(1) walking shoes	Try to find something other than athletic shoes.
(1) nicer slip on heels (optional)	For dressier times in the cities.
(1) belt (optional)	To finish the look.

🧳 Men's Packing List — Spring & Summer

ITEM	RATIONALE
(3) pants: one casual, one dressier, one jeans	You will need the variety.
(2) shorts	Should match with all tops.
(3) T-shirts	For all occasions.
(2) button downs: one long sleeved	Long sleeves are for cooler times.
(1) sweater (optional)	Depends on your preference. Nights can be cool.
(1) poplin jacket or blazer (optional)	For dressier times in the cities.
(5) underwear	Easy to wash and dry.
(4) socks	Cotton is okay.
(1) belt	For a more finished look.
(1) flip flops or other sandals	For relaxing or showering.
(1) walking shoes or hikers	Should match with everything.

🧳 Winter, Cooler Temperatures, Rain Additions

ITEM	RATIONALE
Long sleeves instead of short	Winters are not too cold, but require long sleeves.
Jacket	Will need a light shell or other jacket for cool nights and possible wet days.
Delete shorts, add another pants	If it's warm enough for shorts, you can pick some up at the destination. Typically, you won't need shorts.
Bring slightly heavier fabrics.	The same list can be used by altering the fabrics.
Bring heavier weight for mountain areas.	Higher elevations are always colder. (Also check Rocky Mountains packing list, page 93.)

Sports
If visiting beach areas, don't forget your swimsuit. Other planned sports activities may require packing an additional sports bag.

Colors
Pastels are great in Miami and Las Vegas. Black is good in the cities especially at night. All colors are generally acceptable. Umbrellas may be necessary in the eastern portion of this region.

Style
Casual/Liberal = Countryside
Moderate/Liberal = Most cities
Moderate-Dressy/Liberal = Atlanta, Houston, Los Angeles, Miami

Safety
High to moderate to low (some areas of larger cities have lower safety)

Variable Temperatures
Beach areas are considerably cooler than inland areas in California. Nights can be cold in the winter and in the summer.

Recommended Luggage
- 22" – "26 Pullmans are best.
- Small backpacks are okay if you will be moving around a lot.
- Duffel bags are good for sports equipment, but not recommended for regular travel.

Canada: Central

Alberta, Manitoba, Saskatchewan

Rain & Snow

Most of the rain is in the summers while winters experience a lot of snow. The South can experience warm to hot summers, and the winters are long and cold.

Best Time to Visit: June–August

 Weather by Month

MONTH	GENERAL WEATHER CONDITIONS
January	
February	Very Cold
March	
April	Cold
May	Cool
June	
July	Warm
August	
September	Cool
October	Cold
November	
December	Very Cold

United States: Alaska

Alaska

Rain & Weather

Rain can be heavy on the coasts. Snow and blizzards are likely inland. If going in the summer, a Multiple Climate pack will be necessary. Consult page 141.

Best Time to Visit: June–August

 Weather by Month

MONTH	GENERAL WEATHER CONDITIONS
January	Very Cold
February	
March	
April	Cold
May	
June	Cool, Warm
July	
August	
September	Cold
October	
November	Very Cold
December	

Alaska & Central Canada Packing

People in this region are generally laid back, casual and sporty. There is no need to dress up unless you are going there for a special occasion. Sports enthusiasts will love this area.

Women's & Men's Packing List

ITEM	RATIONALE
(3) pants: one convertible to shorts, one casual, one dressier	You will want pants that can be worn in the wilderness, and in the cities.
(4) T-shirts: two long sleeved	If it's colder, you will need the long sleeves for added warmth.
(2) zipper turtlenecks	Can even be worn in the summers.
(2) sweaters: one heavier weight wool, one medium weight	Some days are warmer than others.
(1) jacket or shell	Provides a top layer to protect against weather.
(1) set long underwear, optional	If going in the winter.
(1) button down, long sleeves	For warmer days or as a layer.
(5) underwear	Easy to wash and dry.
(6) socks, wool	Not too thick.
(1) hiking shoes	Don't bring athletic shoes.
(1) set hat, scarf, gloves	Easy to pack and necessary if it's cold.
(1) warm up suit, cotton	Doubles as pajamas. Good for relaxing.
(1) parka, optional	If going in the winter.

Sports

If you are going to this region for sports, please consult Adventure Packing for cold and cool climate lists, pages 143 and 144.

Colors

Any colors are acceptable with the exception of pastels and white.

Style

Casual/Liberal

Safety

High

Layering

If you use the layering philosophy, you can take this wardrobe any time of year.

Recommended Luggage

- Small Pullmans for city destinations.
- Backpacks for travelers going to the wilderness.

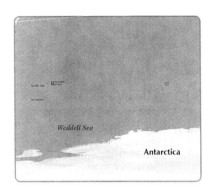

Arctic Regions

Antarctica, South Pole, North Pole

Rain & Snow

There is hardly any precipitation in Antarctica. Extreme weather garments are necessary. Adventure Packing most likely applies, page 143. The South Pole summer is December, January and February. The North Pole summer is June, July, and August. The only time tourists visit is in the summers. It can be sunny, but still cold. The cold is tolerable in the summers.

Best Time to Visit: North Pole, June–August; South Pole, December–February

 Weather by Month

MONTH	GENERAL WEATHER CONDITIONS
January	
February	
March	
April	
May	
June	
July	Very Cold
August	
September	
October	
November	
December	

North America: (Way North), Greenland & Iceland

Greenland, Iceland, Northwest Territories, Nunavut, N. Ontario, N. Quebec, Yukon

Rain & Snow

Little rainfall in this region, but snow is common in winter. Winters are severe and extremely cold. In the South, summers can be mild.

Best Time to Visit: June–August

 Weather by Month

MONTH	GENERAL WEATHER CONDITIONS
January	Very Cold
February	
March	Cold
April	
May	Cool to Warm
June	
July	
August	
September	Cold
October	
November	
December	Very Cold

Arctic Regions Packing

There is no need for formal attire in this region. Adventure clothing is the norm. You will need to pack warm clothing even in the summer. A layering system is the best solution.

Men & Women's Packing List

ITEM	RATIONALE
(3) pants: one convertible to shorts	You may need the shorts on warmer summer days.
(2) turtlenecks	For added warmth.
(1) sweater, wool	Turtleneck sweaters are best.
(4) T-shirts	High tech fabric is best.
(5) underwear	Easy to wash and dry.
(2) bras or sports-bras (women)	Same as above.
(1) set long underwear	High tech fabric.
(1) waterproof rain/snow suit, top and bottom	Will be worn as the shell.
(1) down parka	For cold nights.
(1) set hat, mittens, scarf	Necessary.
(1) mid-weight Polartec™ jacket	For mid layer.
(1) hat (baseball or other)	For sun.
(1) waterproof hiking shoes	Don't bring new shoes.
(1) high tech, light weight button down	Can function as the top shirt over tees and turtlenecks.

Sports
You will probably only be here for some type of sporting adventure.

Colors
Dark colors will absorb more heat.

Style
Casual/Liberal

Safety
High

Cold
If you are not used to the cold, this is not a good place for you.

Layering
If you use the layering philosophy, you can take this wardrobe at any time of year.

Recommended Luggage

- Backpacks are best. Pullmans are not recommended.

North America: Mexico

Mexico

Rain & Weather

Most of the rain falls on the southwest coast from June to July. Southern Mexico is much more humid than the northern region. Desert conditions exist in the North. The inland areas can be very hot year round. Cool nights can be expected in Baja and in higher elevations.

Best Time to Visit: October – March: Southern Region; April – May: Northern Region and Baja

 Weather by Month

MONTH	GENERAL WEATHER CONDITIONS
January	Warm to Hot
February	
March	
April	Hot
May	
June	Hot, Wet
July	
August	
September	Hot
October	Hot to Warm
November	
December	

Central America

Belize, Costa Rica, El Salvador,
Guatemala, Honduras, Nicaragua,
Panama

Rain & Weather

Most of the rain falls between May and October. This area is very hot and humid although there are some cooler areas at higher elevations.

Best Time to Visit: December–March

 Weather by Month

MONTH	GENERAL WEATHER CONDITIONS
January	
February	Warm, Humid
March	
April	Hot, Humid
May	
June	
July	
August	Hot, Humid, Wet
September	
October	
November	Hot, Humid
December	Warm, Humid

South America: Northern Region

Colombia, French Guiana, Guyana, Suriname, Venezuela

Rain & Weather

The rain, from May to October, is frequent and can be heavy. A Multiple Climate pack may be necessary if visiting higher elevations. Consult page 141.

Best Time to Visit: January–February

 Weather by Month

MONTH	GENERAL WEATHER CONDITIONS
January	Warm to Hot, Humid
February	
March	Hot, Humid
April	
May	Hot, Rainy
June	
July	
August	
September	
October	
November	Hot, Humid
December	

South America: Northern Brazil

Acre, Amapa, Amazonas, Bahia, Basilia, Ceara, Mato Grosso, Maranhao, Para, Piaui, Rondonia, Roraima, Tocantins

Rain & Weather

October through April has heavy rain. In the East and South, there is a dry season between May and September. This region is generally hot and humid year round.

Best Time to Visit: May–September

 Weather by Month

MONTH	GENERAL WEATHER CONDITIONS	EXTREME WEATHER WARNINGS
January		
February	Hot, Wet	HEAVY RAIN
March		
April		
May		
June		
July	Hot, Humid	
August		
September		
October		
November	Hot, Wet	HEAVY RAIN
December		

Mexico, Central America, Northern South America Packing

You will enjoy the warmth of the sun, and the passion and generosity of the people in this region. Latino cultures are relaxed and friendly, but not without social guidelines. Casual attire is acceptable. However, when exploring, it's wise for women to wear less provocative clothing than would be acceptable in the beach destinations. (Men, of course, don't have these concerns.) If you are visiting the beaches of Mexico and not planning trips to the interior, follow the packing guidelines for the Caribbean and South Pacific found on page 129. You may also choose to purchase some of your clothing after arriving.

Women's Packing List

ITEMS	RATIONALE
(3) pants: one cargo, one drawstring (loose fitting), your choice	Cargo pants are good for travel days because you can fill the pockets. Drawstring pants are good for hot city days.
(1) light sweater or pullover and/or poncho	Can be cool at night and even rainy.
(2) shorts, not too short, should be walking style	Should not be worn on travel days, but are good for sleeping and relaxing.
(1) skirt	Can be used for dining at night or more formal situations. Since it will not be worn often, it will stay clean.
(3) T-shirts	Tees will get soiled quickly, so taking three makes it easier to keep up with the washing.
(2) camisole/tanks (microfiber)	Works well as an undergarment to keep other clothes from getting soiled.
(3) button downs: one long sleeved, one short	Evenings can be cooler than days, and one top should be able to be worn with the skirt or with the drawstring pants for dressier occasions.
(1) thin, free flowing, long sleeved blouse, easy to wash and quick to dry	Good for keeping clean with the skirt in case you need to dress up.
(1) hat	Good for shade. Should be foldable like a Panama hat.
(4) socks: microfiber, not cotton	Because of the heat, your feet can easily become blistered. Choosing the right socks is just as important as having the right shoes.

🧳 Women's Packing List (cont.)

ITEM	RATIONALE
(5) underwear	Light cotton or microfiber, easy to wash and quick to dry.
(2) bras	Same as underwear.
(1) flip flops	Can be worn for relaxing or showering. Do not wear them on travel days or walking tours.
(1) shoes: good for walking	Don't bring leather athletic shoes! Your feet will swelter. Look for softer, breathable canvas like material. Don't bring new shoes.

🧳 Men's Packing List

ITEM	RATIONALE
(2) cargo pants	Good for all purposes. Some convert to an extra pair of shorts.
(2) shorts	Provides comfort when not on the bus or train.
(4) T-shirts	It's easier to keep up with the washing.
(2) long sleeved all purpose shirts	May be necessary for cooler nights or to provide shade in very hot areas.
(1) pants: chino or other nicer pants	Should be kept clean and not worn often. They come in handy for unexpected dressier situations or emergency laundry situations.
(2) nicer shirts	Same as above.
(1) hat	Provides shade.
(4) socks: microfiber, not cotton	Because of the heat, your feet can easily become blistered. Choosing the right socks is just as important as choosing the right shoes.
(5) underwear	Material should be easy to wash and quick to dry.
(1) flip flops	Can be worn for relaxing or showering. Do not wear them on travel days.
(1) shoes: good for walking	Don't bring leather athletic shoes! Your feet will swelter. Look for softer, breathable canvas like material. Don't bring new shoes, you will be more likely to blister.

Wet Season, Rain Forest, Higher Altitude (Men & Women) — Alterations

ITEMS	RATIONALE
Take out a pair of shorts and/or a shirt. Add a sweater, or lightweight fleece top.	It will be cooler and wetter, but still humid and warm to hot.
Hat should be water-resistant.	You don't want your head to be wet.
Poncho or rain suit, lightweight and thin. Can remove one pair of pants or other item from list above to make room.	You will want to stay dry.
Shoes also need to be waterproof or sprayed with silicon.	Look for lightweight waterproof materials.

Sports
The most likely sports activities in this region are hiking and walking. If you think you will be swimming, add a suit to your wardrobe. Don't swim in fresh water in Guatemala and perhaps other Central American areas because of the possibility of cholera.

Colors
Pastel and whites should not be worn. They will get too dirty. Blues, greens, khakis, tans, all other shades of earth colors are good. Black is okay at night, but not during the day. Everything should match, so you have more choices when combining items.

Style
Casual/Moderate

Safety
Moderate to low
The sun is strong and unrelenting. Good sunscreen and clothing protection is essential.

Rain & Weather
It can remain hot when raining. Also, the rain can bring many bugs. Check local health reports concerning malaria.

Other Notes

If you are traveling by bus, it's important to wear loose fitting pants and long sleeves. First class buses can be cold, and second class buses are hot and dusty.

Always keep your nicer outfit for emergencies. You can neatly pack it in thin plastic wrapping and have it available when necessary. These times may include trips to embassies, visa applications for on-going travel, city dinners, and times when you need to wash your other clothes.

Sleep wear sometimes needs to be long pants and long sleeves because of bugs and cooler nights. If items from the wardrobe cannot be doubled, it's wise to bring designated sleep wear.

Recommended Luggage

- Pullmans are not recommended in this area because there is usually a lot of moving around.

- Small backpacks are recommended.

- Do not bring a large backpack! It's too hot, and you will be miserable.

Caribbean 1

Anguilla, Antigua & Barbuda, Aruba, Barbados, British Virgin Islands, Dominica, Dominican Republic, Grenada, Guadeloupe, Haiti, Martinique, Montserrat, Netherlands Antilles, Puerto Rico, St. Lucia, St. Vincent & The Grenadines, Trinidad & Tobago, U.S. Virgin Islands

Rain & Weather

May typically has the heaviest rainfall. August through November also have more rain. This region typically has warm to hot temperatures, but can also have cool breezes.

Best Time to Visit: December–April

 Weather by Month

MONTH	GENERAL WEATHER CONDITIONS	EXTREME WEATHER WARNINGS
January	Dry Season, Hot	
February		
March		
April		
May	Wet Season	HEAVIEST RAIN
June		
July		
August		RAINY
September		
October		
November		
December	Dry Season, Hot	

Caribbean 2

Bahamas, Bermuda, Cayman Islands, Cuba, Jamaica, Navassa, Turks, Caicos

Rain & Weather

The heaviest rain is typically from June through October. This region is typically hot year round, but is also characterized by cool breezes.

Best Time to Visit: November–April

 Weather by Month

MONTH	GENERAL WEATHER CONDITIONS	EXTREME WEATHER WARNINGS
January		
February	Dry Season, Hot	
March		
April		
May		
June		
July	Wet Season	HEAVIEST RAIN
August		
September		
October		
November	Dry Season, Hot	
December		

South Pacific

Cook Islands, Federated States
of Micronesia, French Polynesia,
Tahiti, Fiji, Guam, Johnston Atoll,
Kiribati, Marshall Islands, Nauru,
New Caledonia, Palau, Palmyra Atoll,
Pitcairn, Samoa & American Samoa,
Solomon Islands, Tarawa, Tokelau,
Tonga, Tuvalu, Vanuatu, Wallis & Futuna

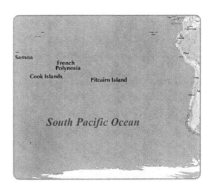

Rain & Weather

The heaviest rain in this region falls in March and April. The South Pacific
region is tropical, but can also have cool breezes.

Best Time to Visit: May–October

 Weather by Month

MONTH	GENERAL WEATHER CONDITIONS	EXTREME WEATHER WARNINGS
January	Wet Season, Hot	
February		
March		HEAVIEST RAIN
April		
May	Dry Season, Hot	
June		
July		
August		
September		
October		
November	Wet Season, Hot	
December		

South Pacific: Hawaii

Rain & Weather

Tropical downpours are common throughout the year. The rain usually clears quickly. It can get very hot in inland areas. The coast can be quite pleasant year round. General weather patterns vary from island to island. Check to make sure you are not planning your trip during the rainy season on the island you plan to visit.

Best Time to Visit: May–November

 Weather by Month

MONTH	GENERAL WEATHER CONDITIONS	EXTREME WEATHER WARNINGS
January	Rain, Mountains	
February		
March		HEAVIEST RAIN
April		
May		
June		
July	Hot, Humid	
August		
September		
October		
November		
December	Rain, Mountains	

Caribbean & South Pacific, Beach Destinations Packing

These beautiful destinations provide the easiest light packing possibilities. The culture provides a relaxed atmosphere, and there are no judgmental restrictions concerning attire. The most popular activities are leisure and recreation, sun bathing, water sports, dining out, night clubbing, and shopping. It's usually easy to buy clothes locally.

Women's Packing List

ITEMS	RATIONALE
(2) pants: loose fitting with drawstring	Can be worn as casual beach attire or dressed up with a blouse for dining or clubbing.
(1) solid color dress for evenings	More colorful or patterned dresses can be bought at the destination. Black is recommended for packing because of versatility and elegance.
(1) skirt	Be sure it matches all your blouses.
(3) camisole/tank tops	Can be worn on their own or under a blouse.
(2) shorts	Useful on the beach as cover up or exploring islands.
(3) T-shirts	Can be used in layering or on their own.
(3) blouses: one long sleeved	Will dress up your wardrobe. Long sleeves for cool nights.
(1) light sweater	Evenings can be cool.
(1) pajamas	Shorts and T-shirts can double as pajamas. In some areas, bugs can be a problem at night. Loose fitting pajamas with long sleeves and pants can be useful.
(1) swimming suit with optional cover up/towel	If you're staying at a resort, you will not need to bring a towel. Other wardrobe items can be used as a cover up such as shorts and tees.
(1) pair of beach flip flops and/or diving booties for wading	Some beaches have sharp coral.
(1) pair of open toed slip-ons	Don't take a chunky heel. A delicate heel is more appropriate. This style is elegant, comfortable, and lightweight.
(5) underwear	Do not bring nylon. The fabric will need to be quick drying.
(2) bras	Same fabric as underwear.
(1) hat	Provides shade. The hat should be foldable such as a Panama hat.

Men's Packing List

ITEM	RATIONALE
(1) cargo pants	Good for exploring in variable weather. Can double as another pair of shorts.
(1) chinos or other slacks	Just dressy enough for dining or clubbing.
(2) dress shirts: 1 short sleeved, 1 long sleeved	Good for clubbing or dining. The long sleeved shirt can be worn on cooler nights.
(2) shorts	For beach walks or on the town.
(3) T-shirts	Can mix and match with other wardrobe items.
(1) pajamas	If necessary. In some areas, bugs can be a problem at night. Loose fitting pajamas with long sleeves and pants can be useful.
(1) poplin jacket	For cool evenings, dining and clubbing.
(1) hat or baseball cap	Provides shade from the sun.
(5) underwear: cotton	Briefs or boxers.
(1) swimming suit with optional towel	If you're staying at a resort, they will provide a towel.
(1) flip flops or diving booties	Some beaches have sharp coral.
(1) loafer type shoes	For dressier occasions.

Wet Season Additions

Please make an effort not to go to these destinations during the wet season. If it's unavoidable, you will need to alter your packing just a bit.

ALTERATIONS/ADDITIONS	RATIONALE
Instead of two pairs of shorts and one pair of pants, take two pairs of pants and one pair of shorts.	It's cooler during this time, and you will stay drier with pants.
Consider bringing slightly heavier fabrics.	Days with rain will still be warm, but nights are much cooler. You can also layer items from the packing list. For example, a camisole, a tee, and a blouse may all be worn together.
umbrella/rain jacket	Most hotels will provide umbrellas, but it may still be necessary to bring an umbrella. A lightweight waterproof jacket like those worn by sailors is also useful.
closed toe shoes	Walking around in the rain with open toed shoes is difficult and uncomfortable.

Sports

If you plan to scuba dive or play tennis/golf, you can bring a separate but small sports bag. If you are using a Pullman suitcase, the sports bag should be able to fit on top of the Pullman. Obviously, if you are an advanced scuba traveler, you will need a larger bag for your equipment.

If you are planning to learn to play tennis or scuba dive, equipment will usually be provided at your destination. Contact the hotel, resort, or dive shop for details.

Colors

The colors you choose for your wardrobe are important. Each item should match. Don't bring an item if it only matches with one other item. This way it's easier to either dress up or down. Colors typically worn at the beach destinations are pastels, light colors, and whites. Black is seldom worn during the day, but can be worn at night.

Style

Casual/Liberal

Dressy/Liberal

It's your choice depending on if you are a dressy person or a casual person. Most tourists will dress casually.

Safety

High to moderate

Tanning

Don't spend more than one hour in the sun on your first day. You will burn. If you burn, you will ruin your vacation. A good rule to follow is 15 minutes on each side, twice. You can increase the time day by day. However, keep in mind that it doesn't take a long time to get a tan in this climate. You will also get a better tan if you do it slowly.

Recommended Luggage

- 22" Pullman: Soft or hard shell is best.
- Small backpacks are fine (not the regular traveler's size, that's too big).
- Small duffel bags are okay, but remember you will have to carry it.

South America: North West

Bolivia, Ecuador, Peru

Rain & Weather

There is not much rain on the coast of this region. However, higher elevations experience rain and snow. The East can be much warmer and wetter than the West. Higher elevations are much cooler than other areas. Weather varies greatly in this region. The table depicts general weather conditions. Be sure you know your itinerary before packing for this region.

Best Time to Visit: Coastal Areas: January–March; Higher Elevations: June–August

Multiple Climate packing is recommended for this region. Consult page 141.

 Weather by Month

MONTH	GENERAL WEATHER CONDITIONS
January	Hot, Wet
February	
March	Warm, Wet
April	Warm, Dry
May	Cool, Dry
June	
July	
August	
September	Warm, Dry
October	
November	
December	Warm, Wet

South America: Southern Brazil & Paraguay

Southern Brazil, Paraguay

Rain & Weather

Rain is heaviest between December and April. In the South and along the coast, it's slightly cooler.

Best Time to Visit: April–June

A Multiple Climate pack, page 141, may be necessary in this region.

 Weather by Month

MONTH	GENERAL WEATHER CONDITIONS
January	
February	Hot, Wet
March	
April	
May	Warm
June	
July	
August	Cool
September	
October	
November	Hot, Wet
December	

South America: South

Argentina, Chile, Easter Island, Falkland Islands, Uruguay

Rain & Weather

The coastal region is dry and warm while the mountains can experience rain and humidity throughout the year. The South is much colder than the North.

Best Time to Visit: November – March

A Multiple Climate pack, page 141, may be necessary.

 Weather by Month

MONTH	GENERAL WEATHER CONDITIONS
January	Hot
February	
March	Warm
April	
May 1–15	Warm
16–31	Cool to Cold
June	Cool to Cold
July	
August	
September 1–15	Cool to Cold
16–30	Warm
October	Warm
November	Hot
December	

South America: North West, South, & Southern Brazil Packing

This region has extreme climates. It can be hot and wet, hot and dry, temperate, and cold. Packing is tricky, but luckily it's casual. Don't wear expensive jewelry or watches because there is a high risk of theft in these areas.

Cultural restrictions concerning dress codes are minimal, however, people do tend to dress up in the cities.

Women's Packing List

ITEM	RATIONALE
(3) pants: one cargo, one drawstring or other slightly dressier (loose fitting). Jeans are okay as long as they are comfortable.	Cargo pants are good for travel days and jungle visits. Some convert to shorts. Dressier pants are needed for nights or city tours. Jeans may be uncomfortable in hot and humid conditions.
(2) shorts	Can be shorter in Brazil but longer elsewhere. Can double as pajamas.
(1) dress or skirt or both	Both are recommended in Brazil. (There is more night life.) The skirt is sufficient elsewhere.
(3) T-shirts	Should match with everything. Can double as pajamas.
(3) camisole/tanks	Can be worn alone in Brazil, but not elsewhere. Can double as pajamas.
(1) long sleeved button down, light fabric	Can be worn for travel days and over a camisole.
(3) blouses: light, short sleeved	Should be free flowing and comfortable.
(1) light sweater, heavier for higher elevations	It can get cool at night.
(1) pullover or other light jacket	In case of unseasonable rain or cold or higher elevations.
(5) underwear	Easy to wash and dry.
(2) bras	Same as above.
(1) flip flops	For relaxing, beach or showering.
(1) walking shoes	Short canvas boots are best. Athletic shoes are not appropriate.
(3) socks	In case it's cold. Should be microfiber.
(1) slip on heels (optional)	For clubbing or dining in Brazil.

ITEM	RATIONALE
(1) hat (optional)	For shade. Hats can be purchased easily at the destination.

Men's Packing List

ITEM	RATIONALE
(3) pants: one convertible cargo, one dressier chino for Brazil, one jeans	Good for all purposes.
(2) shorts	You will wear them often except at higher elevations.
(4) T-shirts	Can double as pajamas.
(2) button downs: one long, one short	Long sleeves will be good for cooler nights. Both shirts should match with everything.
(1) hat (optional)	Provides shade.
(4) socks	Shouldn't be cotton, microfiber is better.
(5) underwear	Easy to wash and dry.
(1) flip flops	For relaxing, beach, and showering.
(1) walking shoes	Should also be able to be worn with nicer chinos. Short canvas boots are better than athletic shoes.
(1) sweater, pullover or light jacket	For unexpected rain or cold or higher elevations.

Winter & Higher Elevations — Alterations for Men and Women as Applicable

ITEM	RATIONALE
Sweater should be warmer	Other items in wardrobe can provide necessary layering. Even Brazil can get cold in the winter.
Shoes warm and waterproof.	It may snow or rain.
Jacket with hood	A shell will provide good protection from the rain, and serve as a good top layer.
(1) set hat, gloves, scarf	In case of extreme cold.
Shorts can be deleted.	If you're not going to be in multiple climates, you don't need shorts.
Blouses and T-shirts	Should be heavier weight.

ITEM	RATIONALE
Turtleneck, one or two	Can be added for areas other than Brazil.
(1) pajamas	Should be warmer.

Winter & Higher Elevations — Alterations for Men and Women as Applicable (cont.)

ITEM	RATIONALE
(1) set lycra long underwear	May be necessary on colder days.
Socks	Should be heavier weight.
Dress and skirt	Can be deleted. May still be taken to Brazil, but needs to be slightly warmer.
(1) blazer or other jacket for dressier occasions in Brazil	In other areas, it's not necessary.

Sports
If you're planning an adventure trip, please consult Adventure Packing, page 143. Swimming opportunities are mainly in Brazil. If you plan to play tennis, or engage in another sport, you can pack a small sports bag.

Colors
All colors are fine in Brazil. In other areas, which may tend to be dustier, earth tones are more suitable. Black can be worn at night. White should be avoided. Pastels are great for Brazilian summers. Winter colors should be darker.

Style
Casual/Moderate
Moderate/Liberal = Southern Brazil, cities

Safety
Moderate to low

The Sun
The sun is strong. Brazil can be very hot and humid in the summer. Near Tierra Del Fuego, there is a hole in the ozone.

Recommended Luggage
- 22" Pullmans are good for Brazil.
- Small backpacks are recommended for other destinations.
- Small duffel bags are okay for sports equipment, but not recommended for general travel.

Notes
The weather tends to be erratic due to increasing elevation.

Accessories

🧳 Necessary Accessories

ITEM	RATIONALE
Hair care products: shampoo, conditioner, brush, comb	If you prefer your own brand, pack your hair care products. Don't bring excessive amounts of sprays and gels. In destinations such as Europe, they sell wonderful products that aren't available in other parts of the world. You may want to try these products.
Toothbrush/ Toothpaste/Floss	Although you can purchase toothbrushes at just about every destination, you may not like the toothpaste. Bring at least a short-term supply.
Lotion	Necessary in drier climates. Depending on your skin, it may not be necessary in humid climates.
Soap, body	Bring at least a short-term supply. It's fun to try new products that aren't available in your home market, so you may want to purchase soap at your destination.
Deodorant	Personal choice. If you don't use it, don't bring it. If you prefer your own brand, bring it. Your brand may not be available at your destination.
Sunscreen	Necessary everywhere. If you choose a good quality sunscreen, it can double as your facial moisturizer.
Sunglasses	Necessary everywhere. Bring only one pair.
Tampons/ Feminine Hygiene	Tampons aren't easily obtainable in most Asian countries. Always bring a supply no matter what the destination.
Razors	Don't bring electric razors.
Cosmetics, make-up	Don't bring excessive amounts. In hotter climates, it will look really bad. Just bring the necessities.
Nail Clipper or Nail File	Can go in cosmetics bag. This is an often forgotten item that's handy.
Swiss Army Knife	For a variety of uses. Don't pack it in your carry-on. It will be confiscated at an airport or border crossing.
Soap, laundry	You may need to hand wash your clothes, but you can easily find laundry soap at your destination. If it will fit in your bag, bring a small supply. Otherwise get it at your destination.
Camera	You will want to preserve your memories.

📦 Variable Necessity Accessories

ITEM	RATIONALE
Water Bottle	If you will be spending a lot of time touring the countryside or trekking, it's a good idea to have a water bottle.
Bandannas	If you will be in a dusty, windy, or very dry climate, bandannas are useful for keeping cool and protecting against blowing dirt or sand.
Bug repellent	Useful for mountain areas and humid, rural areas.
Mini first aid kit and medications	Useful in emergencies.
Towel or shammy	If you don't plan to stay in nicer hotels, you will need to bring your own towel. If you bring a towel, be sure it's thin and quick drying.
Scarves	Scarves are nice for dressing up your wardrobe. If you don't normally wear scarves, don't bother packing them. You will not wear them if you're not used to them.
Jewelry/Watch	One pair of earrings, one necklace, and one watch is enough. Don't bring expensive jewelry. Don't bring anything you can't risk losing.
Belts	If your wardrobe is dressy, you will need a belt. Choose one that can be worn with everything.
Pajamas	Some of the lists include items that can double as pajamas. If you must have separate pajamas, choose pajamas appropriate to the climate.
Purse/Wallet/Coin Purse	For explanations, consult Money, page 161.
Mosquito netting	In areas where netting is necessary, it's often already in the hotel room. Inquire at the places you will stay for more details.
Battery Operated Alarm Clock	Can be very useful when you need to wake up to catch a train, etc. However, you may want to take a watch that has an alarm feature.
Notebook and pen for writing	Useful even if you don't keep a journal.
Books, reading	Don't bring a lot of books. One or two for the plane ride is enough.

🧳 Variable Necessity Accessories (cont.)

ITEM	RATIONALE
Guidebook, maps, phrase book	Try to keep it light.
Swimsuit	If it's not included in the list, it means that the region is not typically a swimming region. However, based on your itinerary and choice of hotel, you may choose to bring one.
Sewing Kit	Useful in clothing emergencies, but may not be necessary depending on your skills.
Binoculars	Depends on the type of trip you are taking. Try to bring small and light binoculars.

Packing Technique Note

You will most likely need everything from the necessity list. You can choose which items you need from the variable list depending on your destination.

Accessories that can spill such as shampoo, lotion, etc. should be packed in zip lock bags. It's handy to have the zip lock bags later for other uses as well. Even maps stay dry in zip lock bags. The zip locks are also very important for keeping clothes dry and clean in case of leaks. Please take note that large amounts of liquids are now required to be packed in your checked baggage.

Towels

Towels can be both useful and a nuisance. If you have to continually pack a wet towel, your clothes will be soiled. Bring an extra plastic bag in case you have to pack the towel when it's wet. Be sure the towel fits into the bag completely. Sometimes it's easy to pick up towels along the way, sometimes it's difficult. If you don't pack a towel, you may end up wasting a lot of time looking for one. Shammies can be efficient in warmer climates.

Electric Hair Dryers & Other Hair Devices

Try not to bring electrical devices. You can often pick up a local hair dryer or curler. Even the appliances that have variable current adaptations do not necessarily work properly in different environments. Consult Hair & Beauty, page 162, for tips on how to avoid carrying around hair dryers and other electrical devices.

Multiple Climate Packing

🧳 Multiple Climate Packing, Women — Hot, Cold, Rainy, Dry

ITEM	RATIONALE
(3) pants: one lightweight, one slightly heavier	Lightweight pants should be cargo or drawstring, heavier pants can be jeans.
(1) shorts	Not too short. Should not be too casual either.
(1) skirt	For dressier occasions in warmer climates.
(1) blazer or other fashionable cover piece	For dressier occasions.
(3) T-shirts: one long sleeved	Long sleeves can provide a layer for colder climates.
(3) button downs or other blouses: two long sleeved	Short sleeves can be worn when appropriate. One long sleeved should be lightweight. The other long sleeved should be slightly heavier for warmth.
(3) camisoles/tanks	Provides diversity in your wardrobe, and provides a good first layer in the cold.
(1) sweater, light to medium weight	Will be good for cooler nights in warmer climates and daily in colder climates.
(1) zipper turtleneck	Can double as pajamas in warmer climates with cool nights, and provides a good layer.
(1) light cotton sweats	Can double as pajamas, and are good for relaxing.
(1) pullover or rain jacket shell	For weather protection.
(2) tights/leggings	Can be worn with skirt or used as long underwear in colder climates.
(5) underwear	Easy to wash, easy to dry.
(6) socks	Light wool or synthetic blends.
(2) bras	Easy to wash, easy to dry.
(1) flip flops or other sandals	For relaxing or showering.
(1) set hat, scarf, gloves	Easy to pack and useful in the cold.
(1) walking shoes	Don't bring athletic shoes. Choose carefully, so the shoes will match all clothing.
(1) collapsible umbrella	In case of rain.

Note

It's best to choose moderate styles for a Multiple Climate pack.

Swimsuit
If you will be swimming or going to the beach, add a swimsuit and/or towel.

Accessories
Consult Accessories, page 138.

Recommended Bag
This depends on the type of trip you are taking. If you will be moving around a lot, a backpack is recommended. If you will be in one place for long periods of time, a Pullman is better.

Multiple Climate Packing, Men — Hot, Cold, Rainy, Dry

ITEM	RATIONALE
(3) pants: one cargo convertible, one warmer	Cargo pants will provide extra shorts. Warmer fabric is necessary for colder climates.
(1) shorts	For hot climates.
(4) T-shirts, one long sleeved	Long sleeved T-shirt will provide a bottom layer in colder climates.
(2) button downs: one long sleeved	Long sleeved shirt should be able to be worn both as a layer and in warmer climates as sun and bug protection.
(1) blazer or other dressier jacket	For dressier occasions.
(1) zipper turtleneck	For added warmth in cold climates.
(1) sweater or other pullover	For cool nights in warm climates and cold days in cold climates.
(1) rain jacket or shell	For rain in warmer climates and a top layer in cold climates.
(1) set hat, scarf, gloves	Easy to pack and useful in the cold.
(1) pajamas, optional	If you do not use other items to double as pajamas, you will need to bring pajamas.
(5) underwear	Easy to wash and dry.
(6) socks	Light wool, or synthetic blends.
(1) long underwear, microfiber	For wearing under pants in cold weather.
(1) flip flops	For relaxing or showering.
(1) walking shoes	Should be waterproof, but not too heavy. Don't bring athletic shoes.
(1) collapsible umbrella	In case of rain.

Adventure Packing

The following items have been chosen for most adventure type trips. Your tour guide may have additional recommendations. A duffel bag is usually recommended for the bag.

🧳 Adventure Packing, Men & Women — Cold Climates

ITEM	RATIONALE
(3) pants	One pair fleece, one lighter weight, cargo.
(4) T-shirts	Preferably high tech fabric.
(1) set long underwear	High tech fabric.
(1) waterproof jacket/pants	Pants with zippers down the sides are best. Zipper jackets are better than pullovers.
(1) mid-weight Polartec™ jacket	Provides a good middle layer. Also doubles as pajamas.
(1) Polartec™ pants	Provides a good middle layer. Also doubles as pajamas.
(5) underwear/(2) bras	Should be easy to wash and dry.
(4) socks	Should be wool.
(1) button down: high-tech, light-weight long sleeved	Can be worn as a light jacket or as an additional layer.
(2) turtlenecks	For extra warmth.
(1) baseball cap or other hat	For sun protection.
(1) parka, mittens, hat	Mittens are warmer than gloves.
(1) waterproof hiking boots	Don't bring new boots.
(4) socks	Warm and dry fabric.

🧳 Accessories

ITEM	RATIONALE
Sunglasses and sunscreen	Necessary.
(2) bandannas	Have multiple uses, can double as wash cloth.
(1) head lamp, 2 extra batteries, 1 extra bulb	For reading at night in a tent or finding your way around in the dark.

ITEM	RATIONALE
Swiss Army Knife	Many uses.
(1) small towel or wash cloth	For showering or bathing.
Notebook, pen and pencil	Pens sometimes don't work in the cold.
Reading materials, small paperbacks	In case you get bored.
Sports cream, first aid supplies, ace bandage	In case you get hurt.
Small containers of shampoo, soap, medicine, vitamins	Don't overload with these items.
Something small and personal to remind you of home.	In case you get lonely or bored.
Camera	You want to preserve your memories.
Binoculars	Optional.

🧳 Adventure Packing, Men & Women — Cool Climates

The following list is for most adventure type trips. The adventure outfitters usually recommend using a duffel bag if you're taking a tour. If you're traveling independently, a backpack is best.

ITEM	RATIONALE
(3) pants: one convertible to shorts	Some days may be warmer.
(4) T-shirts	Can be worn alone or as an under layer.
(1) set long underwear	Can double as pajamas or be worn on colder days as the bottom layer.
(1) waterproof jacket/pants	In case of rain, snow, or cold.
(2) zipper turtlenecks	Can provide extra warmth or be worn unzipped on warmer days.
(1) mid weight Polartec™ jacket	Can be worn alone or as a top layer.
(1) shirt: long sleeved, warmer	Makes a good layer or can be worn alone on warmer days.
(5) underwear/(2) bras	Easy to wash and dry.
(1) baseball cap or other hat	For sun protection.
(1) waterproof hiking boots	Don't bring new boots.
(4) socks	Warm and dry fabric.
(1) lighter shoes	For relaxing and comfort. Athletic shoes are okay.
(1) one hat, spring gloves	May be necessary at times.

🧳 Accessories

ITEM	RATIONALE
Sunglasses and sunscreen	Necessary.
(2) bandannas	Have multiple uses. Can double as a hand towel and protect your neck from the sun.
(1) head lamp, 2 extra batteries, 1 extra bulb	For reading at night in a tent or finding your way around in the dark.
Swiss Army Knife	Many uses.
(1) small towel, or wash cloth	For showering or bathing.
Notebook, pen and pencil	Pens sometimes don't work in the cold.
Reading materials, small paperbacks	In case you get bored.
Sports cream, first aid supplies, ace bandage	In case you get hurt.
Small containers of shampoo, soap, medicine, vitamins	Don't overload with these items.
Something small and personal to remind you of home.	In case you get lonely or bored.
Camera	You want to preserve your memories.
Binoculars	Optional.

🧳 Adventure Packing, Men & Women — Warm to Hot with Variable Precipitation

Keep in mind that fabrics will need to be varied according to the amount of humidity. Duffels are usually the recommended bag if you're on a tour. If you're traveling independently, a backpack is best.

ITEM	RATIONALE
(3) pants: one convertible to shorts	For protection against bugs, snakes, etc.
(3) light button downs: one long sleeved, one short	Long sleeves will provide protection from sun and bugs.
(1) light rain pullover jacket	In case of heavy downpours.
(4) T-shirts: one long sleeved	Long sleeved shirt can double as pajamas.
(1) light weight sweat pants	Can double as pajamas and useful for relaxing.

📦 Adventure Packing, Men & Women — Warm to Hot with Variable Precipitation (cont.)

ITEM	RATIONALE
(2) camisoles/tanks	Good for under layer.
(5) underwear/(2) bras	Easy to wash and dry.
(1) swim suit	Optional, depending on destination and activities.
(4) socks	Not cotton. Light microfiber is best.
(1) lightweight hiking boot	Should not be leather.
(1) flip flops or sandals	For relaxing or showering.
(1) hat or baseball cap	For sun protection
(2) bandannas	Have multiple uses.

📦 Accessories

ITEM	RATIONALE
Sunglasses and sunscreen	Necessary.
Swiss Army Knife	Multiple uses.
Mini first aid: ace bandage, sports cream, bug repellent, medicines, etc.	In case of emergencies.
(1) small towel/wash cloth	For bathing.
(1) head lamp, 2 extra batteries, 1 extra bulb	For reading at night in a tent, or finding your way around in the dark.
Notebook, pen	For writing.
Reading material, paperbacks	In case you get bored.
Small containers of shampoo, soap, etc.	Don't overload with these items.
Something small and personal to remind you of home.	In case you get lonely or bored.
Camera	You want to preserve your memories.
Binoculars	Optional.

Around the World Backpacker Packing

Multiple Climates/Multiple Cultures

This is a difficult pack, but does not require taking a huge backpack. It's particularly important to pack light on a trip such as this. You will be moving around a lot, and you will be uncomfortable if you are carrying a lot of unnecessary items. You can also send items home by slow boat as you change climates. Try not to bring a full sized backpack.

📲 Backpacker Packing, Women — Multiple Climates/Cultures

ITEM	RATIONALE
(3) pants: one cargo convertible to shorts, one dressier, one drawstring, or jeans	Cargo pants should convert to shorts. In many destinations, shorts are not appropriate.
(1) skirt	Length should be past the knee. Should not be too dressy.
(1) shorts	For multiple uses and relaxing.
(3) T-shirts: one long sleeved	For layering or wearing alone.
(3) button downs: at least one long sleeved	Long sleeves are necessary in some cultures.
(1) blazer	For dressing up any outfit.
(3) camisoles/tanks	Good for layering or alone in some areas. (Camisoles cannot be worn alone in some cultures.)
(1) sweater	For cool nights and variable climates.
(1) pullover rain protective jacket	May be used as a top layer in cooler climates and protects against rain in warmer climates.
(2) tights/leggings	Can be worn under pants in cooler weather, and with skirt for a dressier look.
(7) underwear	These trips are usually longer. Should be easy to wash and dry.
(1) swim suit	For beaches, etc.
(1) towel and/or wash cloth	Many backpacker accommodations do not provide towels.

Backpacker Packing, Women—Multiple Climates/Cultures (cont.)

ITEM	RATIONALE
(2) or (3) bras	Easy to wash, easy to dry.
(6) socks	Four light wool or microfiber, two cotton.
(1) set hat, scarf, light gloves	Can provide needed warmth if going from hot to cold.
(1) zipper turtleneck	Useful in cold climates and can double as pajamas.
(1) sweat pants	For relaxing and can double as pajamas.
(1) mid to light weight hiking boots	Best overall style for multiple destination travel. Bring waterproof but not leather.
(1) flip flops or other sandals	For relaxing, beaches, showers, etc.

Backpacker Packing, Men—Multiple Climates/Cultures

ITEM	RATIONALE
(3) pants: one cargo convertible to shorts, one jeans or other casual, one dressier	The cargos provide an extra pair of shorts, the dressier pants are necessary at times.
(4) T-shirts: at least one long sleeved	Long sleeves can double as pajamas and provide a warm layer for warmer climates.
(1) shorts	For warmer climates.
(3) button downs: at least one long sleeved	For dressier occasions, and practical reasons. Long sleeves are good when layering is necessary.
(1) blazer or other jacket	For dressier occasions.
(1) zipper turtleneck	Useful when going from hot to cold.
(1) sweater	Will be a top layer for colder climates.
(1) pullover/rain jacket	Good for top layer in cold and rain protection in warm climates.

🧳 Backpacker Packing, Men — Multiple Climates/Cultures (cont.)

ITEM	RATIONALE
(1) set hat, scarf, light gloves	Good when going from hot to cold.
(1) long underwear, light	For wearing under the pants in colder climates.
(1) light to medium weight hiking boots	Best choice for multiple climates.
(1) flip flops or other sandals	Good for relaxing, showering, etc.
(6) socks	Four light wool or microfiber, two cotton.
(1) swim suit	For beaches, etc.
(1) towel/wash cloth	For bathing.
(1) sweat pants or suit (light)	For relaxing, clothes washing days, and/or sleeping.
(7) underwear	Easy to wash and dry.

Note
You will be able to pick up and delete items as necessary along the way. Don't overload yourself by buying a lot of unnecessary clothing items along the way.

Accessories
Consult Accessories, page 138; Beauty, page 162; and Washing, page 161 for other concerns.

The Business Traveler

Refer to regular packing lists for general weather conditions.

The business traveler can take the same items mentioned in the regular packing lists, but will need to vary the style to suit business meetings. Bringing two suits is usually sufficient for men. Women can bring a blazer, pants, and skirt, with two blouses and mix and match the ensemble to create a variety of outfits.

In hot and humid climates, such as South Korean summers, business attire is still formal. You may want to pack some extra undershirts for excessive sweating.

Those packing for overseas business trips should adhere to cultural concerns, especially women. Choosing appropriate colors is also very important.

Remember that pressing is available at most hotels, so it's not necessary to pack an iron. Check with the hotel before your departure.

Women and also men can use the hotel's beauty salon for hair styling; a blow dry is usually not too expensive. There are also hair dryers in the hotels, so it's not necessary to pack a blow dryer. Check with the hotel before departure.

Laptop computers should be carried on board, and should have secure padded carrying cases. Pay close attention to your laptop as it goes through the airport screening. Some companies now provide their employees with 'clean' laptops – with no personal information or private business data to avoid theft.

Try to take Pullman suitcases. Garment bags are bulky and difficult to carry. Hard side Pullmans are the best because clothes do not wrinkle as much and dirt and moisture cannot get inside.

The lists that follow are designed for average business trips of three to five days. Please also consult Accessories, page 138.

🧳 Business Packing, Women — Spring & Summer

ITEM	RATIONALE
(2) pants	If you don't wear skirts, pack only two pants.
(1) skirt	If you don't wear skirts, delete this item. If you do, pack one skirt and one pant.
(1) blazer	Can be worn with everything. Will provide warmth if necessary.

ITEM	RATIONALE
(3) blouses	In the warmer months, you will appreciate having a fresh change.
(1) light sweater	In case the air conditioning is too cold.
(2) camisoles/tanks	Lightweight, to be worn as an undershirt if necessary.
(2) stockings/hosiery	If one runs, you have a back up.
(2) dress socks	If necessary for your outfits.
(1) comfortable pajamas	Depends on personal preference.
(1) T-shirt	Can be worn when relaxing in your hotel room.
(1) shoes	Try to bring just one pair that matches with everything.
(1) slippers (optional)	For relaxing in your hotel room.
(5) underwear	Can be less if you plan to wash.
(2) bras	Will be needed in warmer climates.

Business Packing, Men — Spring & Summer

ITEM	RATIONALE
(2) pants	Style according to your line of work.
(1) jacket	Style according to your line of work.
(3) shirts	Button downs or other appropriate style.
(2) T-shirts	Can double as pajamas if needed.
(1) shorts	For relaxing in your room.
(1) shoes	Matching with everything.
(5) underwear	Can be fewer pairs if you plan to do washing.
(4) socks	Can be washed easily if you take the right fabric.

Business Packing, Women — Fall & Winter

ITEM	RATIONALE
(2) pants	Should probably be the same color.
(1) blazer	Should match both pants.
(1) jeans	For more casual times and/or relaxing.
(3) blouses	Could even be light sweaters or cardigans.
(2) camisoles	For a bottom layer if it's cold.

📼 Business Packing, Women — Fall & Winter (cont.)

ITEM	RATIONALE
(1) wool sweater	For colder situations.
(1) lycra blend turtleneck (optional)	If you will be at a really cold place, this will make a nice under layer.
(1) top coat	Long, wool is best.
(1) T-shirt	For relaxing in your room.
(1) pajamas	Should be comfortable and warm.
(1) scarf	Easy to pack, and can give an added dimension to your wardrobe.
(1) gloves	In case of really cold weather.
(1) short boots or other shoes	Should match everything.
(2) nylons/hosiery	Can be worn under pants for extra warmth.
(4) socks	For wearing with boots or other shoes.
(5) underwear	Easy to wash and dry.
(2) bras	Easy to wash and dry.

📼 Business Packing, Men — Fall & Winter

ITEM	RATIONALE
(2) pants	Should probably be the same color.
(1) blazer	Suit coat or whichever style fits your profession.
(3) shirts	Cotton button downs or other suitable fabric.
(3) T-shirts	Can be worn under dress shirts for added warmth.
(1) jeans	For casual times and/or relaxing.
(1) sweater or other warmer shirt	For more casual times and/or necessary warmth.
(1) top coat	Long, wool is best.
(1) pajamas (optional)	Personal preference.
(1) pair of gloves and/or scarf	If going to a really cold climate.
(4) socks	Should be warm.
(5) underwear	Easy to wash and dry.
(1) shoes	Should match with everything.

Expatriate Packing

Packing for Moving Overseas, Independent Assignment

This is by far the most difficult pack. If you have not been given a company allowance to ship your belongings, you will have to limit your packing to two check-in bags and one carry-on. As all airline regulations are constantly changing these days, please check the website, www.travelreadypacking.com, for updates and check with your airlines. Difference airlines have different suitcase allowance schedules.

- First, check the packing list associated with your destination.

- Second, confirm the season in which you arrive.

- Third, decide if your destination is formal or casual. Some destinations that are casual for the traveler still require formal work attire.

You will need to focus your clothing pack on the season in which you are arriving. For example, if you are arriving in the European winter, you will pack most of your clothing for winter.

Get the address of where you will be living, or the address of your employer. You can send your other articles by surface mail, and it will arrive in time for the next seasons. (Airmail is very expensive.) Surface mail generally takes two to three months to arrive. Don't pack hair products or other liquid products in a surface mail parcel.

Don't focus only on clothing. There are many other things that you need such as sheets, comfort food, and a comfortable blanket. You will also need space to pack your other necessities.

Don't take styles that you are not comfortable wearing. Your clothes must be comfortable, and you will have to wear the same things again and again.

You can also buy clothing at your destination once you have settled in. However, you will still have to take clothing at least for your first season. If you are a medium to large size, it will be difficult, and probably impossible to buy clothing at any Asian destination.

Consider taking light sporting equipment such as tennis rackets, hiking gear, swimsuits, and others if you are a sports enthusiast. You will find opportunities to do sports, and buying all the equipment can be expensive. Taking ski gear is not recommended because it's awkward.

Trunks are good for packing and can double as a table or computer work station after unpacking. Large rolling duffels also provide a large amount of space. Don't forget to pack a smaller backpack or suitcase in the trunk or duffel. These smaller bags can be used if you take a trip from your new home.

Expatriate Packing Do's

- Take some familiar non-perishable food. When you first arrive, it's difficult to get used to the food. If you have some of your favorite foods, the transition will be easier. Be sure the food you take is sealed and unopened.

WARNING: Some Customs Offices will confiscate any and all food items, sealed or unsealed. This also applies for packing that is shipped via air or sea.

- Spices are also good to bring for cooking, but be sure to pack sealed containers. Don't transport any food items that have been opened.

- Sealed coffee and a small, non-electric coffee maker.

- Take a supply of toothpaste and other toiletry products if you are particular about the brands you use. Also take a supply of your beauty products if you prefer your own brands.

- Women will need to bring a large supply of tampons to Asia.

- Take sheets and towels. These are usually not provided and difficult to find in some areas. It's best to bring flat (not fitted), double or queen sheets since mattress sizes are different.

- Comforter or other blanket. It's nice to have your own comforter. A down duvet packs well and is comfortable. (If you are particular about your pillow, bring your pillow.)

- Take a variety of shoes according to the season. Take at least two pairs of walking/working shoes, and slippers or flip-flops. Others can be sent if you decide to send a surface parcel. In cold climates, it's good to have a pair of boots.

- Take photographs of family and friends in case you get homesick.

- Take a laptop computer if you have one. Carry it with you on the plane. You will be really glad you have it when you arrive. (You may need to purchase a transformer when you arrive.) Also bring surge protectors and necessary wiring for the computer.

- Books are good companions, and can be traded with other expats. Try to bring paperbacks.

- A robe is also an often forgotten necessity. Robes in some areas are hard to find.

- Vitamins

- Medications

- Hair dryers, curlers, etc. If you get a transformer upon arrival, you will be able to use these items. Otherwise, you can buy them at your destination.

Expatriate Packing Don'ts

- Don't bring TVs, VCRs and other such electronic equipment. They are too awkward. You can purchase them at most destinations.

- Don't bring a lot of knick knack decorations for your apartment. They take up valuable space and can be lost. You will be able to find things at your destination.

- Don't bring a lot of jewelry or other expensive items. It's unnecessary.

- Don't bring art-work or other such items. They are too difficult to pack. You can get these things at your destination.

- Don't bring dishes. They are too difficult to pack.

- Don't try to pack all your clothing. Choose the most appropriate and comfortable clothing. Leave the rest behind.

- Don't take sports equipment that you think you might need. Bring only the stuff that you use regularly.

- Don't panic. Everything will work out. If there is something you don't have, you will be able to compensate, or you will be able to find it at your destination.

The Bag

	ADVANTAGES	DISADVANTAGES
Soft	Lightweight Versatile More variable sizes Some are backpacks	Can get wet Can rip or tear Weight distribution is uneven
Hard	Stays dry Keeps clothes less wrinkled Can sit on it Even weight distribution	Heavier Typically large or small only which does not change size.

When Soft?

A soft bag is good for warmer climates where there is not much rain. A soft bag is also good for sports or adventure uses. Whenever the bag has to be carried for long periods of time, it should be a small, soft backpack.

When Hard?

A Pullman is good for destination trips, and trips on which transportation is not an issue. Hard bags are also good for destinations with varying degrees of precipitation. Also, there is less chance of pressure on the contents, so there is less chance of liquid accidents within suitcases. There are many smaller suitcases being made, and a small suitcase doubles as a stool when needed. Hard side Pullmans are best for business travel and European trips for which hotels have already been booked.

Note

A hard suitcase is good for train travel and ship travel (ferries, etc.), and in situations where you don't have to carry the bag for long periods of time. For intense traveling that covers a lot of space and demands a variety of modes of transportation, use a small, soft backpack. Excluding backpacks, don't buy or use a bag that does not have wheels.

Deciding Which Bag Is Right for You

You will have to choose your bag according to the demands of your trip. Analyze your itinerary. If you are going on a trip that requires you to wander around looking for a place to stay or involves ambiguous travel plans, a small backpack is best. If your trip is all planned out with hotel arrangements and transportation, hard side Pullmans are the way to go.

The Size

Less is more. Bring the smallest bag possible. If you plan to buy a lot of clothing or souvenirs, bring an extra empty bag or buy another bag at your destination.

Bag Preparation

Once the proper wardrobe has been selected according to climatic and cultural considerations, the bag is ready to be packed. The way you pack your bag is just as important as the items that go into your bag.

Folding

There are a couple of methods. You can either fold or roll. It depends on the fabrics. In either case, use tissue or plastic dry cleaner bags to ensure against excessive wrinkles. A combination of tissue and plastic is the best. However, if you have to choose one, choose plastic. If something spills in your bag and you have used only tissue, your clothes will get soiled. If you have used plastic, your clothes will remain dry and clean. The plastic bags are also handy for packing dirty laundry during the trip.

Fabrics best for folding

- Linen or linen blends
- Wool
- Silk or silk blends

Helpful Hint

You may have to pack a couple of times to get the weight evenly distributed and/or find the best placement.

Toiletries

Using zip lock baggies helps ensure that any leaking liquids do not saturate your wardrobe. (The baggies are also useful in other circumstances that may arise during your trip.) Items such as blow dryers, curling irons, and electric curlers can often be left behind. (See individual packing tips under your destination.) This not only saves space, but also lightens the load. First Aid items can be neatly packed in their own small bag.

Shoes

Shoes should always be packed in a shoe bag or other plastic bag.

Accessories and Underwear

It's recommended to pack your underwear and socks in a plastic bag. Accessories can all be put together in their own mini-bag.

The Carry-On

The carry-on bag should be smaller than the size recommended by the airlines. On long-haul flights, a carry-on that can double as a footstool can be very useful. These can be small, hard, cosmetic cases or other stable bags that you can place under your feet. It's much more comfortable to have your feet elevated. A small carry-on is important because it lessens the burden of walking around in the airport with a heavy bag. When flights are delayed or canceled, a heavy carry-on will make you more frustrated because you are responsible for dragging it around. A small carry-on is also convenient when browsing in airport shops.

Contents of Carry-On

Check the Transportation Security Administration, TSA, website at tsa.gov for updates, as regulations change frequently. As long as you bring small, travel sizes of liquids and pack them in a clear zip lock bag, you should be okay. It's unnecessary to be excessive.

- Book/Pen/Paper
- Camera
- Important Documents
- Jewelry
- Make-Up/Hairbrush
- Moisturizer/Cleanser
- Toothbrush/Toothpaste

Emergency Change of Clothes

Fit a change of clothes into your carry-on. If your luggage is lost, you will be glad you have it.

On the Airplane

There are many devices and products designed to provide more comfort while in flight. However, take into consideration that you will have to carry these products with you for the duration of your trip. Easy-to-carry comfort products with multiple uses are the best choices.

Aromatherapy products are useful both on the airplane and at your destination. Aromatherapy can help you relax during flight, and can help with jet lag after flights. Be careful about the size of the container, however if you plan to put this in your carry-on.

Small, battery operated massage aids are also very useful on and off the airplane. (Nothing larger than your palm is suggested.)

A good moisturizer is a necessity. Hand cream and face cream should be applied frequently during flight. Be careful about the size of the container, however, if you plan to put this in your carry-on.

For every hour of flight time, it's recommended to drink one glass of water. So, a ten -hour flight would warrant drinking ten glasses of water.

Taking care of your feet during flight is also very important. If you are not wearing slip-on shoes, don't remove your shoes during the flight. Your feet swell. When you put your shoes back on, you will be very uncomfortable upon arrival. If you have to do a lot of walking after arrival, this can be problematic.

Sleeping on the airplane is not a problem for some people. It can, however, be nearly impossible for others. Sleeping is much easier if you elevate your feet or bring along a neck cushion.

What to Wear on the Plane

For long-haul flights, a nice warm-up suit is the most comfortable. For shorter flights, you should just wear the heaviest and most comfortable items from your packing list. Wearing dresses on airplanes can be very uncomfortable especially for long-haul flights. Dresses are fine for short flights, but not recommended for flights over four hours in duration. Closed toe shoes, and natural fibers are recommended for the flight.

Note
If you're taking a long-haul flight, get a moisturizing facial before departure. While on the airplane, do not wear make-up. This way you can apply

moisturizer during the flight. Before arrival, cleanse your face and then apply make-up. It's a good idea to have your hair styled the day before departure. This way, your hair is much more manageable and still looks good after the flight. If possible, try to get a massage before a long-haul flight.

Jet Lag

Jet Lag is a type of fatigue and disorientation caused by a change in time zones, the atmosphere in the airplane's cabin, and/or the physical condition of the passenger. Light deprivation and light over-stimulation may also be determining factors in the severity of jet lag.

Recommendations

There is no cure for jet lag. People are advised to not take caffeine or eat heavy meals before flying. Avoid drinking alcohol before or during the flight. The severity of jet lag also depends on the length of stay: after one year in Asia, I had jet lag for nearly three weeks.

For every hour of time difference, it's suggested that it takes one day to recover from jet lag. A time difference of twelve hours would take 12 days of recovery.

People have varying degrees of jet lag. Some claim to not have it at all. For some people, jet lag becomes worse as they grow older. If you have jet-lag, try not to over-exert yourself. If you feel tired, sleep. If you feel hungry, eat.

Jet lag also affects appetite. Because your body is used to eating according to your schedule at home, you do not feel hungry at the correct times at your destination. Make an effort to adjust your eating schedule, and you will more quickly get on track with the new time schedule.

Some travelers use melatonin to re-regulate their body clocks.

A friend says for flights more than eight hours, she simply goes to bed as soon as she arrives at her destination—no matter what time of day it is—and sleeps until she wakes up. For a 14-16 hour flight, this can mean anywhere from 10 to 18 hours of sleep. When she wakes, she feels completely normal and can easily adapt to the time of day she awakens to.

Note

While some precautions can be taken to reduce the effects of jet lag, it's inevitable in certain circumstances. Try to employ some relaxation techniques, get a massage, drink lots of water, and don't overeat. Mild exercise can also be helpful.

Useful Travel Advice

Laundromats and Dry Cleaners

You can easily take your clothes to the local dry cleaners or laundromats to do your washing. Every neighborhood in an urban setting usually has a dry cleaner and/or laundromat. If your clothes are really dirty, it's recommended to use a washing machine. Washing your clothes in a sink does not always get the dirt out. Many dry cleaners offer to do regular washing as well. In Asia, you can usually find a place that does the laundry for you. Make sure you first ask the price. If you're allergic to laundry soaps, you may want to bring your own soap with you and ask them to clean your clothes with it.

Hand Washing and Drying

Be sure to time your washing with the availability of the items in your wardrobe and the amount of time you will be at the location where you will be washing. If your clothes do not dry in time, you will have to pack them wet. Also be sure that you still have something to wear while doing your washing and during the drying time.

Plastic Bags

Using dry cleaner bags to fold your clothes is best. However, you will also need other plastic bags. Be sure to bring a separate and thicker bag for your dirty clothes. Packing three additional plastic bags is recommended: one for wet clothes if necessary, one for dirty clothes, and one for shoes.

Money

It's best to keep your money in three places. This way, if you are robbed, you will be less likely to lose all your money. A Velcro pouch that secures under a pant leg is a good place to store credit cards, passport, and traveler's checks, and large amounts of cash. You may also want to consider having interior pockets sewn into your travel pants.

A deep front pocket is a good place to store the cash that will be needed on a given day. If you have two front pockets, you can put some money in one pocket and the rest in the other. For women, you can keep some money in your purse. I usually carry my cash on my leg or in my pockets, and put my coin purse in my purse. Don't carry an expensive purse, it will only attract attention. Take a bag that you can keep in front of you, not one that hangs really low or is difficult to hold on to.

ATMs

In some destinations, it's possible to draw money from ATM's. This is a great alternative to carrying cash. However, check with the local tourist office of your destination or with your bank for more detailed information on using your ATM card. You don't want to get there and be unable to withdraw cash. You may also want to provide your bank with your itinerary before you depart. Many banks freeze ATM activity in high-risk countries.

Choosing Your Clothing

You want the most comfortable styles and fabrics. Take clothes that you like. Don't pack culturally inappropriate items. They will take up space and not be worn. Look in your dirty clothes basket and take note of the styles. These are usually your favorite clothes. If you are shopping for new clothes for your trip, take your time. Everything needs to match, and everything needs to be comfortable. Try on many different fabrics and styles. Even if the ones you like the best cost a little more, these are the ones to get. You will not tire so easily of clothes that you really like. Don't take clothes that are too tight, and never bring brand new shoes. If you need to buy new shoes for the trip, buy them well in advance and wear them often before departure.

Hair and Beauty

Women traveling overseas typically have concerns about how they are going to do their hair, especially without a hair dryer. In more conservative and formal societies and in cold weather, it's much more of a concern. In hot destinations, it's easy to just wear your hair up or put on a hat. However, this is not always possible. One alternative is to wash your hair at night, and style it in the morning. However, for people with curly hair, this is disastrous. Go to local salons and get a blow dry. They do a good job, are fairly cheap, and your hair will look great for three days. It's well worth it. You shouldn't bring a lot of make-up, especially to hot and casual destinations. It's likely you will get a tan, and that will be your base. In hot and humid destinations, your make up will run and look really bad. Try to just bring the basic necessities for make-up, such as lip-gloss and mascara. You can also go to a local salon and have a facial. This will help your skin tone and make you feel great.

Hair Dryers and Other Electrical Devices

When traveling to destinations that have different voltages, it's not recommended to bring electronic devices. Even if they have built-in adapters, the products behave differently in varying currents. For example, a hair dryer will blow hotter and possibly burn your hair or even burn itself out. Most hotels provide hair dryers these days. If there is not one in your room, ask the front desk or housekeeping. You can also pick up products locally if you absolutely must have them.

Mistakes and Mishaps

Allow yourself to realize that you don't know how things work in your destination. Mistakes are inevitable. Flights get delayed, and sometimes canceled, hotels are overbooked, etc. Taxis rip you off and drive you around in circles. The list is endless. If you have a light load, I guarantee your frustrations will be lessened. Traveling light, you will be more comfortable and able to deal with mishaps. Remain flexible in your plans. If one thing doesn't work, try something else.

Maps

Do not rely on small maps to get you around. Buy a detailed large-scale map. You will get miserably lost if you try to follow a small-scale map that you have ripped out of a guidebook.

Conclusion

Traveling is a learning experience. Once you have navigated the globe, you have a new perspective on life and living. It takes time to learn the techniques presented in this book, but if you follow these guidelines, you will have a much more enjoyable trip. Please check the website, www.travelreadypacking.com, for updates and new publication releases. It's the author's sincere intention that you will learn to lighten your load and have a great journey no matter where your destination is. Enjoy!

Index of Destinations, by Country

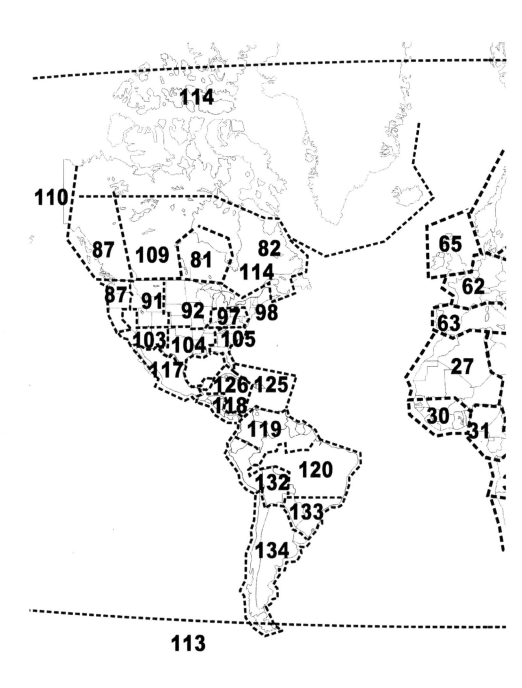

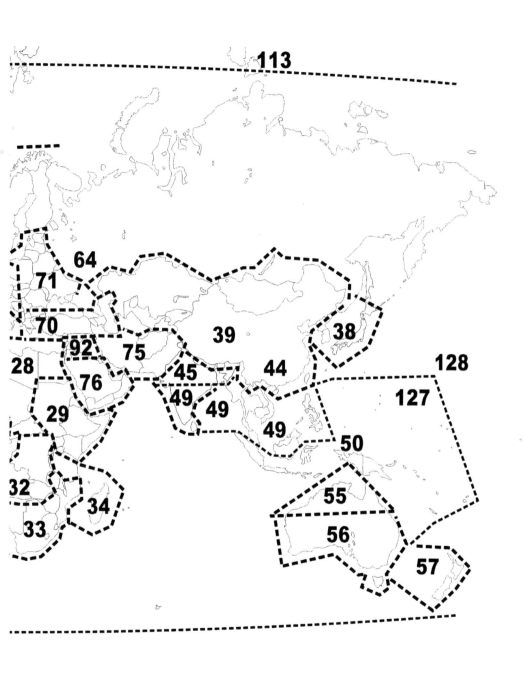

LaVergne, TN USA
26 January 2010
171227LV00008B/35/P